THE
ESSENTIAL
GUIDE
TO
POETRY

David Orme

olens

POETRY POETRY POETRY POETRY

First published 1992 by Folens Limited, Dunstable and Dublin.

Folens Limited
Albert House
Apex Business Centre
Boscombe Road
Dunstable LU5 4RL
England

ISBN 1 85276191-1

CONTENTS

THE PROBLEM SOLVED

- Teachers are sometimes hesitant about introducing poetry into the classroom, perhaps remembering their own experiences in secondary school.
- There is rarely a problem in the primary school. Young children enjoy poems; they enjoy reading them and writing them. They enjoy the rhythms, sounds and patterns of poetry and will often choose a collection of poems in preference to a novel which demands greater commitment. Contemporary 'funny' poets have helped in this process, but children's enjoyment of poems is not limited to comic rhyme. This book contains a range of poems, many by children, that will provide teaching material (and enjoyment!) in themselves.

How do I start a poetry session off?

How can I best organise my classroom to ensure effective writing?

How can I improve the quality of the work my class produce which is so often rhyming doggerel?

How can I cope with drafting and conferencing with a large class?

Where can I get some really fresh ideas?

How much should I be involved in the writing itself?

How can I be sure that the work we do really helps with language development?

These are the questions that teachers ask time and again, and this book sets out to answer them.

Fun with words. Many of the writing activities suggested in this book may not appear to be 'poetry' at all; many of them seem to be merely games with words. All of these activities, however, are designed to give confidence in working with language, enabling children to work with words and try out ideas without the inhibition of a blank piece of paper fill from scratch.

Speaking and listening. The ideas in this book are not limited to *writing* poems. Poetry was seen for many years as a reading and writing activity. We read poems on the page; in secondary schools we wrote *about* them. Writing poems was a separate activity. All of this ignored the possibility of poems as words to be listened to as well as, even instead of, being read. Poems were written in an exercise book; little thought was given to alternative, more interesting ways of presenting them, such as performance. have emphasised these speaking and listening possibilities throughout the book.

Structuring poetry work. Poetry writing is sometimes seen as a one-off, inspirational activity rather than as something developmental and structured. This book suggests a number of ways in which poetry work can be structured and developed, starting with simple ideas, many even suitable for the infant classroom, and developing them into more demanding activities. I have taken as starting points:

- Lists
- Words
- Comparisons
- Patterns
- Sounds
- Narratives
- Ideas are fully cross-referenced so that a number of routes through the book are possible.

I am most grateful to the co-authors of this book, Class 6 at Hiltingbury Junior School, Hampshire, their teacher Pauline Williams and Special Needs Assistant Carol Morris. Their contribution was not limited to trying out ideas and producing poems; a number of the very best ideas are theirs.

SPEAKING AND LISTENING

- Poetry is often regarded as essentially a reading and writing activity.
- This is a pity as poetry, of all the forms of writing, demands close listening and a sense of performance.
- For young children early experience of poetry is entirely auditory, and a sense of rhythm and delight in word play comes entirely through the ear.
- For older children silent reading of poetry should be seen as an extra dimension to, not as a substitute for, listening to poetry and joining in performances.

Reading poetry to children well is an art. Needless to say, reading a poem in the same tone as reading the register will soon bore your audience. The key is to involve the children by *performing* a poem rather than simply reading it out. Use every trick of tone and expression, pitch, volume and emphasis. Be aware of pace and be prepared to vary it and pause when necessary. Use your face and hands, but don't overdo i

What matters most, since we are listening to poetry and not to prose, is that we hear the song and the dance in the words. The dance and the song engage the deepest roots of our minds and carry the poet's words down into our depths. And the final sway over our minds that the poet has, is largely the sway of the hidden waves of song, and the motion of the dance in phrasing of the words that it compels us to share as we read or hear it ...

Reading a wide variety of poems - funny and serious, narrative and descriptive, rhyming and non-rhyming - is vital. However, even with the most spirited performance it is difficult to hold the attention of very young children unless they are involved in the performance themselves, so always include some poems that offer possibilities for children to join in, either by repeating refrains or performing 'actions'. 'A Rainy Day' works well with younger children in both ways.

Children performing. Children enjoy a wide range of reading aloud activities, such as:
A 'reading out my favourite poem' session.
Formal or informal 'choral speaking'.
Reading out work they have written, individually, in groups or pairs.
Preparing a performance for another class or for an assembly.

Rainy Day

'hen Becky woke up she jumped out of bed,
ad a big yawn,
cratched her head,
pened her window, looked out and said:

)h *bother* the rain!'

ot back into bed,
nd went to sleep again.

'hen Becky woke up she jumped out of bed,
ad a big yawn,
cratched her head,
ubbed her eyes, wiggled her toes,
ound her hanky, blew her nose,
pened her window, looked out and said,

)h *bother* the rain!'

ot back into bed
nd went to sleep again.

'hen Becky woke up she jumped out of bed,
ad a big yawn,
cratched her head,
ubbed her eyes, wiggled her toes,
ound her hanky, blew her nose,
atted her tummy and licked her lips,
ut on her dressing gown, did up the zip,
pened her window, looked out and said,

)h *bother* the rain!'

ot back into bed
nd went to sleep again.

4

When Becky woke up she jumped out of bed,
Had a big yawn,
scratched her head,
Rubbed her eyes, wiggled her toes,
Found her hanky, blew her nose,
Patted her tummy and licked her lips,
Put on her dressing gown, did up the zip,
Found her slippers under the bed,
Opened her window, looked out and said ...

'It's stopped raining!'

5

So she
Had a big yawn,
scratched her head,
Rubbed her eyes, wiggled her toes,
Found her hanky, blew her nose,
Patted her tummy and licked her lips,
Took off her dressing gown (undoing the zip)
Took off her slippers and looked for her sock,
Put on her vest and her new summer frock,
Jumped down the stairs, opened the door,
ran into the garden, and guess what she saw:

A great big black cloud just ready to pour!

'Oh *bother* the rain!
I'm going back to bed again!'

David Orme

Performance notes

1. Teacher to read and perform actions.
2. Teacher to read and perform actions. Some children will naturally join in at this stage. Pause after 'looked out and said' and allow children to provide the response.
3. Ask the children to perform the actions while the teacher reads.
4. Ask the children to do the words and the actions this time. Prompt if necessary. They will, of course, get the refrain line wrong which adds to the fun!
5. Children do actions this time, at double speed!

Learning poems by heart. In every case children need some opportunity to rehearse their reading. Talk about the way it should be spoken, the appropriate number of voices, how the poem breaks down into sections. Often, children will be encouraged to read out from their early drafts, and they may well have problems reading their own writing! Reading out written work is best regarded as part of the final, presentational stage; any reading aloud from 'work in progress' is best left to the teacher. When asking children to learn poems, ensure:

■ *There is a clear purpose; a performance, for example.*

■ *Children have some involvement in the choice of poems.*

■ *Children are not pushed beyond their capabilities.*

■ *Children with learning difficulties are asked to 'share' a poem, learning only perhaps a line or two. Their contribution will be just as valid.*

CHOOSING POEMS FOR CHILDREN

- There are many good poems particularly suitable for children, but no good poems that are *only* suitable for children.

Children are all too well aware when they are being talked down to. It is important, therefore, that a very wide variety of poems are made available, including those apparently too difficult for them.

POEMS SHOULD BE:

- Available in a range of anthologies, posters, poetry cards, and cassette tapes. A single 'class anthology' inevitably limits the available choice, but it does make it possible for the whole class to read a poem together, which is one of a range of useful activities. Given a tight budget, two copies of a range of anthologies is the wisest choice for a class poetry library.
- Displayed. This can be a mix of work by children, and by adult poets.
- Performed to the class by the teacher or other pupils. Teachers should be prepared to offer children their own favourite poem. This should be a genuine choice, even if the poem is a difficult one.
- Listened to on tape, in performances, perhaps by the poets themselves.
- Shared. Encourage children to share their favourite poems.
- Read. Allow time for quiet reading. Children enjoy reading poems over and over again. Do not discourage this.

Snails

Sound of snails - crying,
Sound drifting through the brush,
sound of crying.
Slime of snails, dragging
themselves
Along the low-lying plain, crying;
Snails with their slime, crying.
Sound drifting through the bush:
dragging themselves along,
crying.
Snails, their sound blowing
overhead from among the
bushes.

If children are to become fluent and expressive writers, they need to be exposed to a wide variety of writing styles, including poetry. Their work is patterned by close encounters with a diversity of texts so that they assimilate different styles and unconsciously reproduce them in their own writing often at a much later date. They need time to absorb and reflect on what they read so that it becomes part of themselves.

Understanding Snails. Try this poem with your class. Ask them, as a start, to illustrate it.

■ Adults sometimes have problems with this poem, seeking out hidden 'meanings' or symbolism which they cannot find.

■ One ten-year-old told me: 'That's just like me on my way to school in the morning!'

■ This child knew, instinctively, that what this poem required was an *emotional response*, **not** an analytical one.

■ The search for *meaning* as a priority response bedevils poetry teaching at all levels; it should not start in the primary school.

■ Young children can respond to a wide range of supposedly 'adult' poetry in their own way.

Note: *Snails* is a translation of an Australian Aborigine song.

A class poetry library should contain:

- A range of modern poems, including 'funny' material and more thoughtful items. Children love comic doggerel, especially if it is subversive and rude, but they will be sold short if this is the only poetry available.

- Poems using rhyme and metre, unrhymed poems, shape poems, songs and other performance poetry.

- Traditional or 'classic' poems of the English canon, such as 'The Pied Piper of Hamelin' and 'The Lady of Shallot'.

- Poetry from a wide range of cultures, including poems in dialect.

- Anthologies of poems written by other children.

- Poetry cards and posters.

ENJOYING NARRATIVES

- One of the traditional purposes of verse was to tell a story.
- With the establishment of a new oral tradition in recent years many good narratives have been written that work well with children.

For younger children, ensure that some of the classroom picture books tell their story in poetry. For older juniors, there is a wide range of possibilities, from 'classics' such as 'The Pied Piper of Hamelin' (Browning) 'The Inchcape Rock' (Southey) 'The Charge of the Light Brigade' (Tennyson) Sir Patrick Spens (Anon) and 'The Highwayman' (Alfred Noyes) to the streetwise humour of Michael Rosen and Roger McGough.

The storytelling tradition is particularly strong in the Caribbean, and much exciting narrative poetry comes from poets who have links with this region. Look for poems by Grace Nichols and John Agard.

For younger children a narrative needs to be simple, and contain strong repetitive elements.

Grandpa's Toffees

Grandpa was feeling hungry.

'Becky' he said, 'Will you go down the shop,
And buy me some toffees with nuts on the top?
The ones in green wrappers in a jar on the shelf;
Here's a pound coin;
Keep the change for yourself.'

So Becky got ready. She first tried to think
Where she'd last had her shoes
(They were under the sink)
She opened the door,
Stepped over the cat
(It never would move; it was lazy and fat)
Pulled the door shut and went down the path
To the gate that squeaked
like a cow trying to laugh
Into the street and right round the bend,
Past the chip shop, the cake shop,
and on to the end
Near the hole in the road
They were starting to mend ...

And just as she thought she was fed up with streets
She got to the shop that sold grandpa's sweets!

She opened the door and went into the shop.
'A bag of the toffees with nuts on the top,
The ones in green wrappers, they're up on the shelf
And two sherbet dabs on a stick for myself.'

BUT...

'I'm sorry my dear I've sold out of those sweets.'
She went out of the shop (She hated those streets)
Past the hole in the road they still hadn't mended
The cake shop, the chip shop (that road never ended)
Opened the gate that laughed like a cow
Climbed over the cat
(It was fatter still now)
Opened the door and took off her shoes
Went in to Grandpa and told him the news.

OH ...

'I'll have a bag of the plain ones then.'

So Becky got ready. She first tried to think
Where she'd thrown down her shoes
(They were under the sink)
She opened the door,
Stepped over the cat
(It never would move; it was lazy and fat)
Pulled the door shut and went down the path
To the gate that squeaked
like a cow trying to laugh
Into the street and right round the bend,
Past the chip shop, the cake shop,
and on to the end
Near the hole in the road
They were trying to mend ...

And just as she thought she was fed up with streets
She got to the shop that sold grandpa's sweets!

JT ...

...e got chocolate or raisin
...e pink ones are treats,
...t I'm sorry my dear I've sold out of those sweets.'

...e went out of the shop (She hated those streets)
...st the hole in the road they still hadn't mended
...e cake shop, the chip shop (that road never ended)
...ened the gate that laughed like a cow
...mbed over the cat
...was fatter still now)
...ened the door and took off her shoes
...ent in to Grandpa and told him the news.

...H ...

...I have the pink ones then.'

...o Becky got ready. She first tried to think
...here she'd thrown down her shoes
...hey were under the sink)
...e opened the door,
...epped over the cat
...never would move; it was lazy and fat)
...lled the door shut and went down the path
...o the gate that squeaked
...e a cow trying to laugh
...to the street and right round the bend,
...st the chip shop, the cake shop,
...d on to the end
...ear the hole in the road
...hey were trying to mend ...

...nd just as she thought she was fed up with streets
...e got to the shop that sold grandpa's sweets!

..., bag of pink ones please.'
...ertainly, madam. I'm sure you'll like these.'
...he gave him the money and picked up the sweets
...'ent out of the shop (She hated those streets)
...st the hole in the road they still hadn't mended
...ne cake shop, the chip shop (that road never ended)
...pened the gate that laughed like a cow
...limbed over the cat
...t was fatter still now)

Opened the door, took the shoes off her feet
Went in to Grandpa and said 'Gramps, have a sweet!'
He took one from the bag, put the rest on the shelf,
And said 'They're delicious! what sweets
Did you get for yourself?'

OH ...

She'd forgotten to buy the sherbet dabs!

'Well, pop down and get them' he said.
'No! because ... I'm fed up with going. I'll have some of
yours!'

David Orme

Many of the narratives suitable for older children lend themselves to a range of follow-up work on narrative. The work should be speaking and listening based.

■ Children, in groups, should ask their own questions, and make their own discoveries about the poems.

■ What happens next ...? (Stop reading the poem half-way through and ask children to predict the outcome.)

■ Retell the story in a different setting: the 'Pied Piper', for example, could be someone who has come to the school to get rid of the cockroaches.

■ Tell the story as a comic strip or wall frieze.

■ Make a list of the questions children would most like to ask the characters in the poem.

■ Develop a board game from the strong narrative events.

■ Make a tape of a dramatic performance.

■ Create a front page newspaper about the narrative in the poem. RODENT OPERATOR IN CHILD ABDUCTION SCANDAL!

Children will:
- take different roles, e.g. Pied Piper and Reporter
- interview the imaginary characters about events, their thoughts and feelings
- write up the articles - or use a computer
- illustrate the page
- create the entire newspaper.

Extension ideas on 'Grandpa's Toffees'.

■ *Tell the story in pictures.*

■ *Perform it. You will need people to play Becky and Grandpa. Groups could make the sweetshop and a representation of the street. A group can be mending the road.*

WRITING

- The role of the teacher has changed dramatically over the years. For far too long the teacher was not seen as playing a part in the creative process itself.
- The teacher provided the writing stimulus, then responded in one way or another to the writing produced.
- There is a growing realisation now that this strategy is not enough, and does not provide the best opportunity for development to take place.

Now the teacher is seen as a vital part of the writing process, taking on some or all of the following roles:

✓ Providing an appropriate setting and atmosphere in which purposeful writing may take place.

✓ Building confidence in handling language and ensuring a successful outcome for the child.

✓ Helping pupils towards a discovery of writing possibilities in their own lives.

✓ Involving him/herself in the writing process to a degree appropriate to the needs of the class and the individual child.

✓ Providing the opportunity for children to present their work effectively.

It is now generally accepted that there are processes to be demonstrated and taught for writing. These processes are shown in the diagram.

> I found myself being *a supervisor* and this was no good. When I became *a writer* with my class, the children saw that I faced the same problems as them. Suddenly it became *real*; poetry was something that grown-ups *did*. This was not just another school exercise.

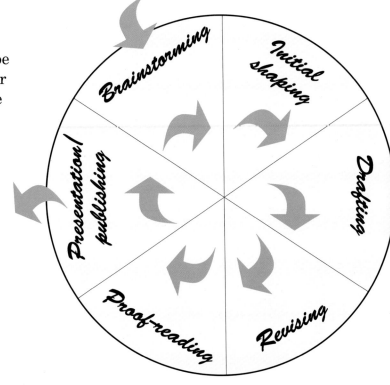

Some ideas will seem unformed or silly. Rather than reject them, ask the child to think about the idea and maybe develop or modify it. Occasionally, an idea will have to be discarded, but point out to the class that all writers have to sort out their best ideas from the less good ones, but without the less good ones no one knows what the best ones are!

■ Give some guidance. You might call for a list of interesting verbs, for example. Children enjoy the challenge of being given a specific target; 'Think of ten words to describe the way an elephant moves.'

■ Participles are a good way in to verbs; ask for 'ing' words. In the shaping stage, the 'ing' can be dropped:
'The Elephant lumbered' is stronger than 'The Elephant was lumbering.'

■ In the early stages, with a class unused to brainstorming, be involved by filtering, suggesting, contributing. As their confidence grows, your help will become less and less necessary.

Brainstorming. Our aim should be to enable children to quickly accumulate ideas, words, and phrases to use as the basis for the writing task in hand. It is a task requiring considerable confidence; many children are initially worried about putting down something 'wrong'. Teachers are sometimes obsessed with ideas of neatness and the right answer. These principles direct you and the child away from what poetry is really about. Neatness and correctness come later. Start with class brainstorming sessions, in which the teacher accumulates the ideas of the class on a board.

■ When managing the class brainstorm, obviously, order must be kept, and the usual 'hands up' rule will allow the teacher to control the situation and allow the quieter members to contribute. These approaches have been found to be helpful:

■ Suggest that children note down their ideas while waiting their turn. This will prevent the sudden blank face of the child who has forgotten what he or she was going to say, and also allow them to keep thinking during the brainstorming process.

The end result is what I call a 'Poetry Stockpot'. An example is on page 26. This is a strategy for collecting together all the words and ideas in order that the children can use them in their writing.

■ As confidence grows, children will be able to produce their own 'stockpots', in groups, in pairs, or by themselves.

GROUPWORK

REWARDS

✓ It encourages co-operation and problem solving through discussion.

✓ It allows less able pupils to be supported and enables them to play their own valuable part.

✓ It aproximates to a 'real-life' work situation.

✓ It develops speaking and listening skills.

PROBLEMS

✗ If over-used, it can become too much of a routine; some children work better by themselves and enjoy the opportunity to do so.

✗ Unless the teacher is careful, the weaker children can be swamped by the more forceful. Democratic processes can be set up to ensure everyone has a chance to contribute, but this is not always easy to monitor.

✗ Ultimately, writing, as any art form, is largely a matter of individual inspiration. Co-operative learning is of enormous value at the learning stage, but, in the end children need the confidence to 'go it alone'.

There is a variety of ways in which groups can be structured, and it is worth trying a range of approaches.

SIZE

Try varying sizes, between three and six.

MEMBERSHIP

A regular group allows children to work with a team they are accustomed to and work well with, but vary this pattern from time to time for variety.

ABILITY

Mixed ability groups have a number of benefits. It is also valuable to allow an able group to be stretched by working together or with a teacher as an enrichment activity. A weaker group can be usefully helped by the teacher becoming a member of the group.

THE GROUP AT WORK

One member of the group should be given the task o 'scribe'. The scribe writes down the ideas of other members of the group as well as contributing ideas of his or her own. This task should be rotated, although clearly there wil be problems for the very weak or slow child.

Ten rules for working in groups

1. Try to get on with the people in your group
2. Take it in turns to speak
3. Don't just accept everything everyone says
4. If you disagree, say so but remember to say something nice about what the other person has said
5. Ask questions if you don't understand
6. Explain well, keep to the point and make things clear
7. Say things which help others
8. Don't butt in - wait until the other person finishes
9. Share your suggestions and ideas with the rest of the group
10. Speak up but don't boss others around.

Encourage members of the group to spend the first few minutes of their group brainstorm session making notes individually and silently. When the discussion starts, suggest that they continue to make notes; this will reduce the temptation to interupt others.

The teacher should be on hand to help the group, perhaps by suggesting ideas from other groups, or by initiating a new line of thought.

In secondary schools much use is made of groupwork when pupils are given a new poem to read. The informality of group discussion often reaches the heart of a poem in a way that a teacher-led discussion or written appreciation exercise cannot. This approach can be adapted for younger children. Ask each group, for example, to choose a poem to prepare and read to the class, explaining why they chose it.

Children should learn to reflect on their own performance and development to become self-critical.

■ *Within the context of the group this can be done by asking the children to review what they have done - perhaps by listening to their performance on tape, or by hearing the comments of peers - and to comment on what has been learned, to report back to the teacher or to share their thoughts with other groups and compare their thoughts with those of others.*

■ *They can also be asked from time to time to comment on the performance of the group as a whole, on how well individuals contributed and to consider how performance could be improved.*

PAIR OR INDIVIDUAL WORK?

- The funnel approach is a useful model for primary writing.
- As the children gain more confidence with their writing, there will be more emphasis on work 'lower down' the funnel.

The aim ultimately of the funnel technique is for children to be sufficiently confident in the various stages of writing to produce finished pieces of work on their own. The 'funnel' provides necessary support on the way.

Teacher and the whole class

PAIRED WRITING

Paired writing brings many of the benefits of groupwork, and ensures a greater level of contribution from each individual.

As with groups, teachers need to keep an eye on how the pairs are formed. Children will wish to work with a friend, and boys will rarely elect to work with a girl and vice versa. An occasional rearrangement of the pairs can bring useful variety.

Groups

Pairs

Individual

Most of the writing activities suggested in section five of this book will work with any grouping: class, group, pair or individual. There are some, however, that are particularly suitable for writing 'turn and turn about' in pairs.

■ **The question and answer poem.** The idea is to write a poem as a series of questions and answers. 'If it wasn't' poems are an example:

> Why is water wet?
> *If it wasn't, we could never have a bath!*
> Why is the sun hot?
> *If it wasn't, we'd all live in igloos!*
> Why is grass green?
> *If it wasn't, cows would starve because they wouldn't know what to eat!*

■ **The conversation poem.**

> 'I want an ice-cream'
> *'Well, you can't have one.'*
> 'Why not?'
> *'Because I say so.'*
> 'But WHY not?'
> *'I've told you!'*
> 'No you haven't, you just said "Because I said so".'
> *'Well, that's why.'*
> 'Why?'
> *'Why what?'*
> 'Why can't I have an ice-cream?'
> *'Oh, for goodness sake, go and get an ice-cream. Anything to shut you up!'*

This can be usefully used to help with the teaching of speech marks!

Conversation with a poem. In this activity the writing partner is a poem! Start by introducing a poem, a line at a time on a board or chart and asking the children what they think about the line and what is going to happen next. In this way the children can work up a dialogue with a poem.

Summer grass aches and whispers
I've never heard it whisper!
It wants something
I've never heard it beg
It calls out and sings
What does it sing?
It pours out wishes
Pours like water?
To the overhead stars
Millions of miles?
The rain hears
It must have good ears
The rain answers
What does it say?
The rain is slow in coming
Slow as a slug?
The rain wets the face of the grass
The grass becomes water.

■ **Creating a story.** A combination of question and answer and conversation can form a story. A marvellous model is the anonymous ballad, 'Edward':

'Why does your sword so drip with blood,
Edward, Edward?
Why does your sword so drip with blood,
And why so sad go you O?'

'O I have killed my hawk so good,
Mother, mother,
O I have killed my hawk so good,
And I had no more but he O'

Unspeakable Revelations

'Why is your wallet so stuffed with cash,
Edward, Edward?
Your wallet's so fat I call it a cheek
When I've nothing left at the end of the week,
And now your credit card collection is almost unique,
O how do you do it, Edward, Edward?'

'I rob building societies and banks, mother;
With my stocking mask and my sawn-off shotgun
I pinch the money and run, Mother
I pinch the money and run!'

Chain poems. *In chain poems, one word from each line must be used to start the next one off:*

It's a really hot day.
Hot enough for ice-cream to melt before people can eat it.
People are squashed together on the beach,
Together we splash in the sea,
See how my arms are turning brown!

(Cheating, such as that in the last line, is to be encouraged!)

GET STARTED - WRITING FOR REAL

- There is no substitute for real experiences in writing.
- All too often, however, children are asked to write on topics outside their experience, or to write on issues in a vague, generalised way.
- This sort of writing is unlikely to be productive.
- A request for a poem on ozone depletion, for example, will rarely produce more than slogans, vague outrage, and platitudes, while writing about the impact of, say, traffic or urban decay in the children's own street or community can produce really genuine writing.
- Even TV or photographs can only provide a 'second best' experience.

The hamster doesn't die every day! Traumatic events can lead to genuine writing, but, mercifully, these do not happen very often! All teachers will be aware that the best writing comes out of a 'need to write', to capture a real event on paper. The problem is that the need to write does not come on demand. This is true for professional writers as much as for school pupils. Holidays, visits, bonfires, family events, traumatic or otherwise, and so on all provide regular, (and sometimes over-predictable) source material for writing, but how can we extend this list to encompass a wider range of possibilities?

Children looking under the terrapin.

The key lies in extending children's sensitivity to the writing possibilities in their own lives, by encouraging them to see familiar experiences such as shopping, playground games, the journey to school, and so on, in new ways; *to make the humdrum special.*

Once pupils are used to this idea, they will bring their own observations and experiences into the classroom, along with the usual contributions for the nature table.

Under the Terrapin. A 'Terrapin' is a variety of temporary prefabricated classroom in wide use in UK schools. Mark, Michael, Laura and Francesca talk about how a chance observation led to writing.

Some of us went to see the differences between Mr Wilton's terrapin and our new one. While we were doing this, we spotted a large hole in the side of the old Terrapin. Some of us borrowed a torch and had a look.

There was so much rubbish under the terrapin we immediately thought of a 'dump'.

When we looked we saw a crisp packet leaning on a brick, and it looked like a slide. It reminded us of a fairground. Because our topic was change we were always thinking of changing things!

We saw two bricks with a stick jammed between, like a floodlight. The bricks looked like stands, so we decided to write a football match poem.

Of course, inspiration, a good idea, will not lead to poetry in itself. The basic idea is established first of all: rubbish and insects under the terrapin.

Next children brainstorm the topic - associations, words, ideas.

Now decide what it is most like, e.g. 'A fairground'.

A conferencing session on this piece of work focussed on the use of particles - 'ing' words - and drafting can then begin.

You can follow this procedure with any topic to explore images and develop concepts of simile and metaphor.

■ *These sorts of real experiences are not damaged by working at them in this way.*

■ *Drafting and polishing can get nearer to what the children felt about an experience and make the experience special by preserving it.*

Final version

Fairground Under The Terrapin

Glow-worms lighting up the fairground
Woodlice whizzing round the octopus body
Millipedes rushing to buy a hot dog
Ants becoming impatient to climb on the big wheel
Roller-coaster going up and down
Hedgehogs twirling round on the helter-skelter
Dodgems crashing into one another
The spiders creeping to the amusement arcade
Mice scaring each other in the haunted house
Badgers slipping down a slide
A big queue for the candy stall
Suddenly the sky turns black
Rain seeps in
Water rises
Fun and dreams are washed away.

Caroline, Faye, Helen and Laura

POETRY AROUND US

- Children listen to and read poetry all the time - they just don't realise it.
- Poetry from the world around us can provide a cheap resource and a host of ideas for starting to write.
- In this format, important poetry skills can be easily incorporated into classroom topic work.

If poetry can be defined as 'language patterned to achieve a particular effect', then children can be made aware that poetry of various kinds is to be found in the world around them.

Too often, children come to believe that poetry is just something that is 'done in school' and is not a part of their life — of their direct, day-to-day experience. This section should prove that this is not true.

It is easy to show that listening to the world around them and keeping their eyes open are easy ways of appreciating and assimilating poetry and its techniques.

HUMPTY DUMPTY sat on the sill
Humpty Dumpty had a big chill
All of his efforts to heat up his pad
Went out the window, and that made him sad.

Double glazing using our 'K'
Keeps those silly chillies at bay,
It's coated, it's clear, it bounces back heat
To warm up the home, not warm up the street.

Humpty Dumpty sits on a rug
Humpty Dumpty's snug as a bug,
Even on grey days he's warmed by the sun
Glazing with K's the best thing he's done.

AMAZINGLY PAYS IN YOUR GLAZING!

All the suggested activities in this section can be easily adapted and developed by children as emergent writers.
- Collections of 'found poems' can be made.
- Surveys can be carried out into the various kinds of poetry around.
- Examples of each can be written, so practising important poetry skills:
  - rhyme
  - rhythm
  - repetition
  - sounds of words
  - layout of poetry.

EPITAPHS

NEWSPAPER HEADLINES

PLAYGROUND CHANTS

RHYMES IN GREETING CARDS

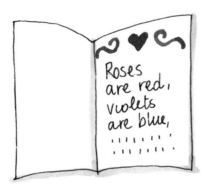

ADVERTISING SLOGANS

SONG LYRICS

GRAFFITI

JOKES AND TONGUE TWISTERS

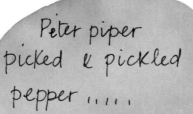

These 'found' ideas can be continued and developed to:
- make chants
- be used as refrains
- be used as writing models.

MEMORIES AND PEOPLE

The suggestions elsewhere in this book give the idea, perhaps, that writing can only take place when an appropriate experience fortuitously comes along. This is not the case; there is much useful work that can be teacher directed. A rationale for the 'word-game' approach appears on page 24. The best writing comes from applying the knowledge acquired in trying out a range of language activities to *real experiences*.

It is perfectly possible for teachers to engineer *real* experiences, which do not have to be dramatically exciting ones.

The experience may be something as simple as bringing an animal or an unusual object into the classroom, or even asking the class to look out of the window at the weather!

Remember, too, that memories hold a rich store of experience which can be called on for writing.

Using memories. Before attempting this children will need a 'recall' session, in which they talk about the experience they are to write about.

■ A few judicious questions will suggest possible ideas for inclusion.

■ The recall will need to be jotted down as a 'brainstorm' - this is a good activity for pairwork, where the 'scribe' makes notes for the 'recaller'.

■ The results of memory poems can be interesting, but beware of expecting children to feel nostalgic, or to respond to nostalgic poems; this seems to be an emotion limited to adulthood!

■ There are a range of activities in this book where memories can be used; in particular, see the work on narrative (page 18).

A Funny Two-Year-Old

When I was two my brother was four.
I was filling the paddling pool with water.
I had a hose in my hand,
And my brother
Ran and pushed me in!
I think I was crying, Wah!
Everyone was laughing, Ha Ha!
Mum was a bit worried I think,
But Dad was nearly crying because HE
thought it was so funny.
I hated them ALL!

Laura

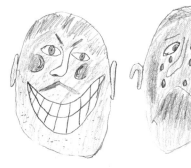 

The Absent-minded Teacher

Children need time - time to develop the confidence to find their own poems inside themselves. We may trigger off the process of remembering, reflecting, but the best ideas are already in the children. It's just patronising to think they have nothing to say. If we insist on proposing what in essence are our poems, we are in effect teaching them that their ideas, experiences and feelings are not the right stuff for poetry.

Writing about people. 'Other people' is probably the most important experience in our lives. Unfortunately, writing about people can be a dismal exercise:

My best friend is called Sarah. She is 10. She wears glasses and has dark hair. She is 1 metre 28 centimetres tall and has brown eyes. She likes pop music and ready-salted crisps ...

A more fruitful approach is to start with a story-telling session, in which children relate an anecdote about the person they are describing. The best of these will reveal far more about the character described.
Using approaches suggested in this book this source material can be shaped into character poems, then displayed with 'head portraits' of the person described.

'Where is it?
Where is it?
Under the table?
Under the carpet?
In the drawers?
In the books?
Where is it?

Where is it?
It isn't anywhere!'
(Mrs Williams was tidying
up her desk and lost
her staple gun.)

'We can't find it anywhere!
Have you looked in your bag?'
'Er ... no ...'

WHAT a surprise!

Lucy

WORD GAMES

This section may seem to contradict what has been said previously in this book; word games hardly count as writing based on *real* experience.

(handwritten words radiating from a drawn sun: heatwave, dazzling, Phew!, shining, Brilliant!, I love the sun!, We go brown, Summertime, on the beach, Swimming, Screwing up my eyes, melting, hot, lazy)

Real experience, though does not make poetry by itself. That experience has to be turned into *language*, and word games are an excellent way to start building confidence in using language. The process of writing can be summed up in this way:

Observation, experience, empathy + Language skill and technique
= Poetry

Many of the activities suggested in this book are word games of one sort or another. The ideas on these two pages are good starter exercises.

Weather words. Collect together words, ideas and phrases connected with particular weather and use them in a display.

RAIN words can be written individually in rain drops or on an umbrella

WIND words can be written on the sails of windmills, or on bending tree branches

SUN words can be written as the rays of a sun.

And so on. The words discovered can be built up into poems, perhaps by using a short refrain:

> Huff! Puff!
>   blowing and roaring,
> Huff! Puff!
>   pushing trees over,
> Huff! Puff!
>   making windmills go round,
> Huff! Puff!

■ **Simple verb games.** Make up a Noah's ark poem with the children, asking them to fill in the words in the gaps:

> Here come the elephants, ... along,
> Here come the kangaroos, ... along,
> Here come the sparrows, ... along.

This game will inevitably produce participles or 'ing' words. These are not as strong as other verb forms so this variation will break that pattern:

> Here come the elephants, they . . . . . . along.

It is valuable to try both approaches and for children to notice differences between using 'ing' words and others.

Acrostics. This is a familiar exercise in which the subject of the poem is written vertically to form the first letter of each line:

Curled up
Asleep by
The fire,
Snoozing...

Extend these a little by using an activity or movement rather than an object:

Up flies the
Plane, far

Away.
No one knows its
Destination;

Do you want to go
Over land and sea
With me, and
Never come back?

Cloze poems. Poems are offered with some words, phrases or even whole lines missed out. The object is not to find the original - the 'right answer' - assuming there is one, but to come up with an interesting range of possibilities. A starter such as:

The sea roared like
A . . . . . . grey . . . . . .

can be a useful lead into talk about similes.

Leave out the verbs or nouns. Missing out adjectives is usually less productive. Obviously silly possibilities will be offered - allow these at first, to get them out of the way! Even these though might promote discussion of more technical points such as imagery and rhyme.

Cut up poems. *Short poems can be copied, then cut up into individual words. The task is to arrange them, not necessarily in the original order! This is particularly interesting if words from two short poems are mixed together.*
■ *Longer poems can be cut into lines or stanzas for sequencing - good practice at developing narrative skills, as well as producing often surprising results.*

Some would argue against drawing children's attention to the use of 'poetic devices' on the grounds that it interferes with the natural flow of their words and thoughts but the evidence is that, far from hampering children, an introduction to the ways of proficient writers does nothing but good. Those who have tried their hands at the tricks which contemporary poets have invented and used and who are encouraged to fit their voices to a wide range of poetic forms, will become confident writers, well prepared to take poetry with them as they mature and develop.

- With drafting a great deal of input is needed from the teacher at first.
- Children need to work collaboratively initially to develop confidence.
- Pupils are sometimes reluctant to redraft and often when they do so they only attend to superficial elements.
- Redrafting is hard work; children need to be enthusiastic about the subject in order to follow the process through.
- Secretarial skills should be ignored at this stage.

DRAFTING - INITIAL SHAPING

The aim of a brainstorming session is to produce a *Poetry Stockpot* of words, ideas, and phrases that might be useful for the job in hand. I suggested there that a class brainstorm should be structured and shaped by the teacher, either by setting targets (10 verbs to describe ...) or by judicious filtering and questioning. Once children are used to brainstorming as a class they will be able to carry over those skills into working in groups or pairs, or by themelves.

This 'stockpot' was produced on the chalkboard during a class brainstorm on WIND. The different colours were used to distinguish groups of ideas - verbs, images, things that happen when the wind blows, and so on. Rings and arrows are used to make links. Once the stockpot is complete, the process of drafting can begin.

Coalescing. In this approach, the ideas in the stockpot will gradually join ·gether by a process of trial and error, until a atisfactory first draft is achieved. This is a pod approach when the subject is non- equential, as in the windy day poem in hand.

'Big Bang'. For poems with a more equential content, perhaps involving arrative, the 'Big Bang' approach is worth ying. The idea is to get down, as quickly as ossible, the series of events. This might be y:

- Using a cassette recorder to 'tell the story'.
- Writing the story quickly as a short prose piece.

/hat is produced will be the first draft. There much more detail on this approach later in e book; see pages 79-81.

FIRST DRAFT

Beware! Beware!

The wind sounds like an invisible town
crier, breathing heavily,
Brings a draught to your spine.

BEWARE! BEWARE!

Trees tapping at the window
Like bats knocking at the door.

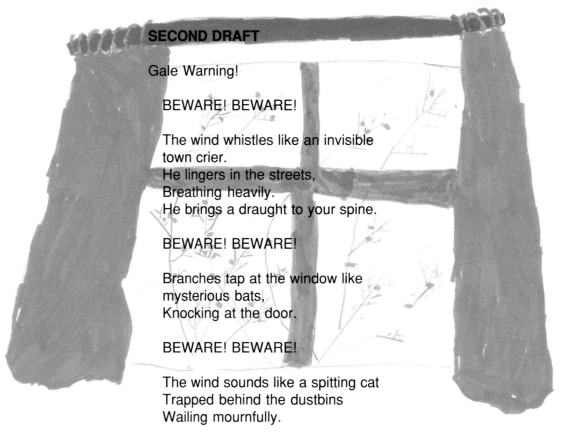

SECOND DRAFT

Gale Warning!

BEWARE! BEWARE!

The wind whistles like an invisible
town crier.
He lingers in the streets,
Breathing heavily.
He brings a draught to your spine.

BEWARE! BEWARE!

Branches tap at the window like
mysterious bats,
Knocking at the door.

BEWARE! BEWARE!

The wind sounds like a spitting cat
Trapped behind the dustbins
Wailing mournfully.

Poetry workbooks. *If possible, keep an exercise book or notebook especially for poetry writing. Use the back for brainstorming and drafting, and the front for finished poems. This encourages children to consider drafts as important and not to be discarded when the poem is finished.*

■ *Word processors.* *Drafting on screen cuts out a great deal of tedious rewriting and appeals very much to children although their word processing skills need to be quite sophisticated. Remember that if children are unfamiliar with using a keyboard, writing will be a frustrating process; drafts cannot be preserved.*

DRAFTING: FIRST DRAFT TO FINAL POEM

- It is important that the teacher is involved in the drafting process, although with the ultimate aim of developing in children the critical judgement and technique to revise their own work.
- As the children become more confident, teachers will need to be involved less and less.
- The key is TRUST: children must trust teachers to help them but not 'take over' their poem.
- This trust must start early; drafting develops as writing develops, from early in the infant classroom. It should not be introduced as a 'topic' later.

The 'drafting conference' sounds good in theory, but in a class of thirty or so children there are practical difficulties in offering each pupil a reasonable conference time, and in occupying other pupils who need help simultaneously. These suggestions may offer solutions

✓ Even a brief conference can be valuable. Don't try and tackle every possible point; pick on one or two learning points that might be usefully developed.

✓ Don't get bogged down in the secretarial aspects of error correcting at this stage. Accurac is important, but even professional writers leave detailed proof-reading to a later stage.

✓ Encourage conferences between writing pairs. Children can be shrewd and sometimes les inhibited critics of each other's work than the teacher!

✓ Provide a list of drafting points. The one on page 29 is suitable for older children with some experience of poetry; it can be simplified and adapted for younger children.

The object of a conference is not to turn the child's poem into the teacher's, but to find out what the child wants to say and help her/him to say it better. Always start a conference by inviting the child to talk about the poem and the experience that led to it. Ask questions! This process of talk will help make the experience that much clearer in the child's own mind.

✓ Be positive. Pick out parts you particulary like, perhaps by highlighting them with a highlighter pen. Ask which part the child is particularly pleased with.

✓ Ask if there any parts that the child isn't quite happy about and would like help with.

✓ Offer just one or two suggestions, not as instructions but as possibilities to be considered.

✓ If the child is having difficulties, be prepared to help with starters, first lines, contributions to the 'stockpot'. Better this than a chewed pencil and a blank piece of paper. It is vital to build confidence at an early stage.

Drafting games. Activities such as cloze procedure and lineation exercise help with drafting, and examples of these are included in this book.

■ Another possibility is the class draft. Find an early draft of a poem, such as the wind poem in this section, and work on it with the class. Using a poem by a member of the class can cause problems, and this should b avoided until sufficient trust has been built up

FINAL VERSION

Gale Warning

The strong wind's dark voice
Is an invisible town crier,
Who lingers in the streets,
Breathing heavily,
Bringing a draught through your spine.

BEWARE! BEWARE!

Branches tap at the window
Like mysterious bats
Knocking at the door.

BEWARE! BEWARE!

The wind's sharp voice
Is a spitting cat,
trapped behind the dustbins,
Wailing mournfully,
Bringing a chill to your heart.

Conferences stimulate children. They stimulate because the child does not work. Children teach, solve problems answer impossible questions, or discover new information hidden in the recesses of experience. The children can do this when their teachers know it is the child's action that produces the learning.

POETRY DRAFTING CHECK LIST

1. Read your poem through. Think. What did you want to say? Do you think you have said it?

2. Words. Are there any words you are not happy with? Underline them and ask for help. Are all the words necessary? Can you get rid of any words?

3. Comparisons. Are there any interesting comparisons and unusual word pictures in your poem? Would this help?

4. Rhyme. If you have used rhyme, do all the rhyming words make sense? Do the rhymes make the poem better?

5. Patterns. Have you written to a special pattern? Have you got the pattern right?

6. Lines. Have you thought about where your lines end?

7. Punctuation. Have you used punctuation? Are your sure your choices are the right ones?

8. Ending. Does your poem have a good ending or does it just fizzle out?

9. Listening. Does your poem sound right? Read it out to someone. Underline any parts that don't sound right.

10. Proof reading. Have you given your poem a final chech for spelling and accuracy before you copy it out?

By Claire Dickel

THE GHOST

The Ghost of Hadleigh Ca
Roams round on windy nig
Off shore his boat is mo
Ready to bring the contr

Some say the ghost has p
Others say he looks rea
Some people say, you go
And the Devil holds full

The drafting checklist can be adapted and offered to children, either as:
- a class poster
- as a list for inclusion in their poetry writing book
- as separate cards.

■ It is not proposed that children should stolidly work through the list before bringing the poem up for inspection - this is unrealistic. It is useful as a reminder and as something a teacher can quickly refer a child to during a conference.

MAKING LISTS

- Making lists is a simple way for children to assemble words and ideas and build vocabulary.
- It is also a fundamental part of brainstorming.

List writing can be developed into the idea-web discussed in 'Poetry Stockpot' (Page 26). The lists can be assembled by the class working together with the teacher scribing, in groups, pairs, or by individuals.

Stage 1: accumulating words/phrases/ideas, however unlikely.
Offering a target number can be helpful:

- 'Think of at least ten things you buy from the supermarket.'
- 'Tell me all the things you can do on a sunny day.'
- 'What ten things do you know about hedgehogs?'
- 'Write down eight words that describe what chips taste like.'
- 'What six noises would you hear on a busy town street?'

Stage 2: selecting.
With young children, most of the words and ideas will be included. As children progress, they will need to be more selective. A useful instruction is to ask children to put a tick next to their best idea or ideas. Encourage children not to erase or cross out rejected ideas, but to see them as material for possible future writing.

Stage 3: patterning and ordering.
Writing, especially poetry, is patterned language. Look for links in the material you have accumulated.

Picture captions. A simple way to use your lists is to display them in patterns on the page, either as collage picture captions or as part of the design to make PICTURE POEMS.

■ **Possibilities for picture poems:**
- Jungle scene with animals.
- Underwater scene.
- Busy street (with noises).
- Fireworks with words rather than sparks.
- A washing line with words and phrases flying in the wind instead of washing.
- Snake poem - the snake ideas are linked end to end to make a snake around the classroom.

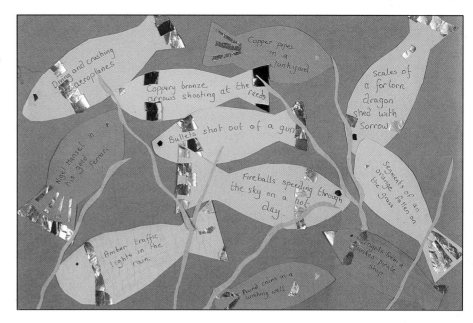

Anything goes' is the starting premise in getting children to respect their own impressions, tap the wealth of self and discover their power over words, their power to create and make meaning.

Other links. The links might be sounds, such as repeated letter sounds or rhymes:
- *Apples and avocados.*
- *Bread and beans.*
- *Custard and cabbages.*
- *A jar of jam.*
- *A piece of cheese.*
- *An instant whip.*
- *Some frozen peas ...*

■ *The ideas can be patterned by describing their purpose:*
- *Flour to make a Christmas cake.*
- *Cherries for Mum's favourite trifle.*
- *Packets of crisps for our lunchbox ...*

NUMBERS

Numbers are a useful way to provide a pattern for list poems.

These poems are ideal for learning by heart and reciting.

A chorus can be added, and each time the poem is read another item is added, or taken away.

A popular game is to line up ten children, who read out 'Peter's Pets' in turn. The child at the end of the line has to make up an animal (or make the sound of the animal for the class to guess). This child then goes to the beginning of the line, and everyone moves down a position.

These sorts of list poems begin to develop rhythmic patterns. This idea can be developed further. (See 'Rhythms and Raps' page 74.)

■ **Number patterns.** Numbers can go down as well as up. A pattern such as the chorus of 'The Twelve Days of Christmas' can be adapted for a list that gets smaller and smaller.

Supermarket poems. The supermarket purchases, for example, might be listed in the order in which they were bought:
- FIRST in the trolley goes bread and eggs,
- SECOND a tin of sausage and beans,
- THIRD some cakes and chocolate buns ...

■ Or the quantities of the various items.
- ONE jar of jam, full of strawberries,
- TWO cucumbers, long and green...

■ Why not add in the colour? ...
- THREE bananas, all in a bunch,

■ Or even pictures ...
- FOUR tasty on toast ...

full of strawberries

long and green

all in a bunch

tasty on toast!

Peter's Pets

In his bedroom, Peter kept
TEN earwigs that scuttled and hid,
NINE spiders that wove their webs,
EIGHT white mice with little pink eyes,
SEVEN hampsters that snoozed in their cage,
SIX black cats, who were after the mice,
FIVE big dogs, under the bed,
FOUR pigs, lazy and fat,
THREE pythons who hung from the light,
TWO donkeys who lived in the wardrobe,
and ONE ... GUESS WHAT?

Ten Little Schoolchildren

10 little schoolchildren
standing in a line
one opened her mouth too far
and then there were 9

9 little schoolchildren
trying not to be late
one missed the school bus
and then there were 8

8 little schoolchildren
in the second eleven
one twisted an ankle
and then there were 7

7 little schoolchildren
trying out some tricks
one went a bit too far
and then there were 6

6 little schoolchildren
hoping teacher won't arrive
one flicked a paper dart
and then there were 5

5 little schoolchildren
standing by the door
one tripped the teacher up
and then there were 4

4 little schoolchildren
longing for their tea
one was kept in after school
and then there were 3

3 little schoolchildren
lurking by the loo
teacher saw a puff of smoke
and then there were 2

2 little schoolchildren
think fights are fun
one got a bloody nose
and then there was 1

1 little schoolchild
playing in the sun
whistle blew, buzzer went,
and then there were none!

Trevor Millum

Poetry is the prime forum for playing, for turning words upside down and making them your own; it frees you from the awesome and complex conventions of language usage yet lures you into dabbling in them, by the same token befriending and conquering them.

Time poems:
- At ONE o'clock we ...
- At TWO o'clock we ...

Speed poems:
- At TEN miles an hour we ...
- At TWENTY miles an hour we ...

Variations:
n 'Ten Green bottles' and 'Ten in the Bed'.

ACTIVITY POEMS

- **Good, active verbs are essential for the writing of activity poems.**

This section deals with two kinds of activity poems - those dealing with imaginary activities.

Activity poems start by accumulating a list of actions connected with a particular activity. The activity might be:
- Cooking or other household chores.
- Playing a game of some sort.
- Activities on a farm or in a factory.

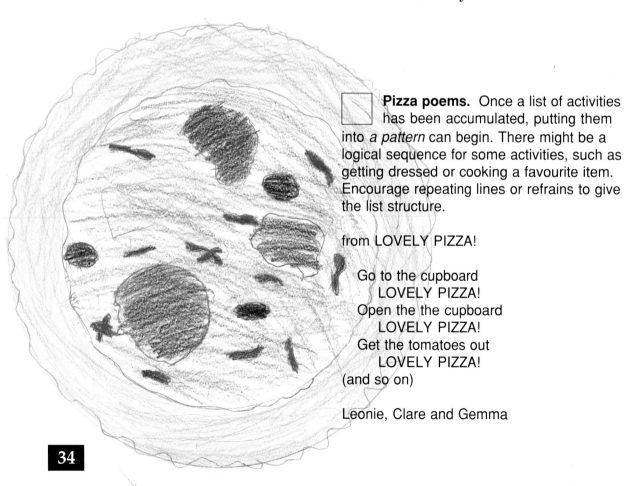

Pizza poems. Once a list of activities has been accumulated, putting them into *a pattern* can begin. There might be a logical sequence for some activities, such as getting dressed or cooking a favourite item. Encourage repeating lines or refrains to give the list structure.

from LOVELY PIZZA!

Go to the cupboard
   LOVELY PIZZA!
Open the the cupboard
   LOVELY PIZZA!
Get the tomatoes out
   LOVELY PIZZA!
(and so on)

Leonie, Clare and Gemma

■ **Performance.** Writing poems in the imperative in this way can turn our list into an action poem. Children will need to develop mimes for each of the actions, each to be performed by a group. Once the class has worked on an action poem, groups can work together on their own, to perform to the rest of the class.

■ **Impossible activities.** This idea is based on the famous poem by John Donne, of which this is an extract.

Go and catch a falling star,
Get with child a mandrake root,
Tell me, where all past years are
Or who cleft the devil's foot,
Teach me to hear the mermaids singing,
Or to keep off envy's stinging,
And find
What wind
Serves to advance an honest mind.

There are a range of possibilities, including lists of impossible actions the writer would like to carry out if only it were possible:
- Lists of awful instructions for a 'hate' poem.
- Nagging 'I told you so' poems.
- Lists of difficult or impossible challenges like John Donne or the labours of Hercules.

Double Dare Poems.

ouble Dare

WHY DON'T YOU ... climb up the outside
of the Statue of Liberty?
WHY DON'T YOU ... dig through the Earth
to Australia? (And back again)
WHY DON'T YOU ... blow the leaning tower
of Pisa down?
WHY DON'T YOU ... pretend you're
Superman and run head first into a wall?

raig, Stewart, Matthew, Craig and Oliver

hicken if you don't

Go on, jump off the Empire State Building.
    CHICKEN IF YOU DON'T!
Go on, hang glide into the sea.
    CHICKEN IF YOU DON'T!
Go on, eat a cactus.
    CHICKEN IF YOU DON'T!
Go on, jump into a volcano with no clothes
    on.
    CHICKEN IF YOU DON'T!

raig Griffin

> Writing a poem is as easy (or as hard) as you care to make it; it makes its own rules; it is unique. So long as a poem carries the tiniest scrap of yourself with it, it will always stand up, it will always have worth.

Yarns. 'They Have Yarns' by Carl Sandburg is an interesting poem to use for extension work.

They have yarns
Of a skyscraper so tall they had to put hinges
On the two storeys so as to let the moon go by.
Of one corn crop in Missouri when the roots
Went so deep and drew off so much water
The Mississippi river bed that year was dry.
Of pancakes so thin they had only one side.
Of a fog 'so thick we shingled the barn and six feet out onto the fog'.

■ *Children could use one of the yarns and write it as an illustrated story. If they try to treat the yarn seriously, they will soon learn that it will seem even more ridiculous.*
■ *Lastly, they could invent their own yarns:*
  - *They have yarns of the teacher who shouted so loud ...*
  - *They have yarns of the boy who had a tongue so long ...*
■ *Optical illusions. These provide a useful stimulus for poems concerning impossibilities. Try the work of M C Escher.*

EXTENDING LISTS

Lists provide a simple and enjoyable way of building poems from an initial brainstorm. They can be an end in themselves, or can be developed into poems of considerable subtlety and power.

Ingredients for a Spell to turn beautiful frogs into ugly princesses.

Ants feet
    (old and dried)
Toad legs
    (boiled and fried)
An early bird
    (Stir it up well)
A mouldy snail
    (Still in its shell)

Adam

Some of the most resonant passages from the Bible are in the form of lists. 'The Properties of a Good Greyhound' is a medieval example of a list poem. It provides an interesting model for writing, as do the other poems on these pages.

What the teacher has in her desk!

In the teacher's desk, you can find:
A set of keys with gruesome faces staring at you
Two hairy, horrid spiders
scuttling across the remains of a rotten, brown apple.

And ...

Three piles of unfinished lines
Four bitten pencils with small bits of filling on them
Five thumbs in five, large thumbscrews!

Lucy

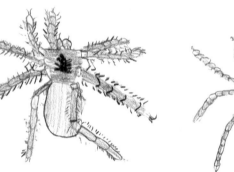

In my wonderful world

In my wonderful world
No one would be hungry
No one would start wars
No one would be greedy
No one would make pollution
Who will share my wonderful world?

Martin

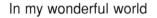

It is a good idea to begin to include abstract ideas in the list poems as well as concrete objects. These last two examples mix the concrete and abstract to make poems full of surprises.

It is possible for children to cut, edit, reject and abandon large chunks of their writing on the creative way to something succinct and true. Brevity of form demands as compensation a high quality of concentration. Far rather the telling ten-liner than ten pages of verbal flab.

The Properties of a Good Greyhound

A greyhound should be headed like a Snake,
And necked like a Drake,
Footed like a Cat,
Tailed like a Rat,
Sided like a Team,
Chined like a Beam,

The first year he must learn to feed,
The second year to field him lead,
The third year he is fellow-like,
The fourth year he will avail
Great bitches for to assail,
The eighth year lick ladle,
The ninth year cart saddle,
And when he is comen to that year
Have him to the tanner,
For the best hound that ever bitch had
At nine year he is full bad.

Dame Juliana Berners

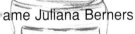

What I'd put in my nasty corner

In my nasty corner I'd put
Spinach
    Ten to two a.m.
Being quiet

In my nasty corner I'd push
Doing the washing up
    Going to bed
Cabbage

In my nasty corner I'd throw
School dinners
    Tidying my bedroom
Assemblies

In my nasty corner I'd kick
Coming to school
    Mushy peas
Paying for things!

Charlotte and Debbie

My magic box

In my magic box I would put

A dog
    Happiness
        money

No war
    sweets
        no taxes

A horse
    kindness
        A hamster

Nice clothes
    Peace
        Sky TV

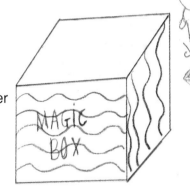

Faye, Matthew, Helen and Laura

FINDING THE RIGHT WORDS

- 'Finding the right word' is a central part of writing poetry, but the phrase covers a range of activities including:
- A word to express the particular shade of meaning intended. English is a language rich in synonyms.
- A word that can mean more than one thing, perhaps to act as a pun.
- A word with a range of associations.
- A word that is surprising because of its unexpectedness in a particular context.
- A word to fit a particular grammatical or structural context - a rhyming word, for example, or a particular verb or adverb.
- Made up words or word combinations: see nouns.
- Examples of all these activities can be found in this section.

The poet may be looking for precision; on the other hand, much poetry is deliberately ambiguous, and there is often more to individual words than meets the eye!

The ideas in this section extend the 'word games' mentioned on page 24 and suggest ways of extending them into poetry.

Collocation. This game throws unlikel words together to see what happens!

■ Start with a range of ADJECTIVES and NOUNS. Make sure that some abstract noun are included. Write these on slips of paper and place them in 'bran tub' containers, one for adjectives and one of verbs.

■ The idea is to pull out one slip from each 'tub' and see what ideas the two words suggest. This is quite a difficult exercise and so it is worth working through one as a class discussion. The two words do not necessarily have to be used in the final poem, but might simply suggest a theme. GREEN and ANGE might provoke, for example, a poem about th writer's feelings about damage to the environment.

■ An extension of this is to add an extra tub, containing VERBS. These tubs suggest word to start you off.

Of course most words will fit in at least two lists; many will fit in all three with minor changes. Discussion of this is very useful for children's knowledge of how language works. For older children, encourage them to mix the lists; deliberately to use the words from the noun or the adjective tub as verbs, for example. Ask them to discuss the meaning of these verbs:
- to machine
- to feather
- to ghost
- to green.

■ All do have real meanings as verbs, but they can also suggest a range of unusual writing possibilities.
■ A good way to start the writing process is with the noun - Feather.
Then look for the describing word - Green feather.
Then a verb to describe the action - Green feathers crumble.
■ Not all the process need be random; once the noun is established, children can be allowed to scan the lists for words that appeal.

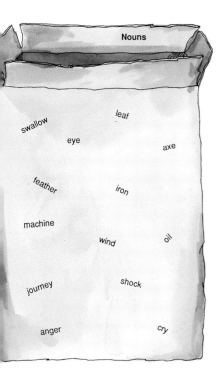

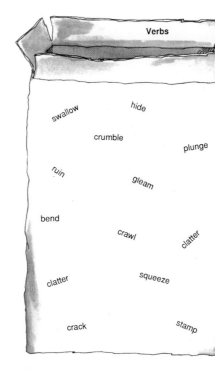

Computer poems. *No one will convince me that computers can write poems! However, like an infinity of monkeys, the computer is good at throwing up random combinations of things so unlikely that no one would have thought of them. There are a number of randomising programs that produce these lists automatically and have the additional bonus of being more impressive (and, of course, expensive) than the 'low tech' bran tubs suggested above.*

■ *Wordstrips.* *Children can make their own randomising program with strips of paper and card. Nouns, verbs, adjectives and phrases can be written consecutively on strips of paper and pulled through display slots. Poems have to be made from the strange juxtaposition of ideas, e.g. 'I like to wear sticky computers!'.*

THE THESAURUS GAME

A thesaurus is a vital item in any classroom and a range of these is available suitable for a range of levels. A simple version of the game that follows works well with quite young children.

The children arrive at school on a cold morning. How many words can they think of to describe how they feel?

■ The following collection might be abstracted from the class. One possible way to set out the words is to use a spider diagram:

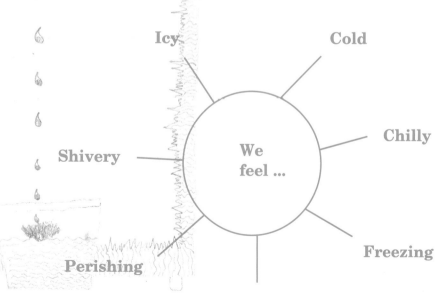

Icy

Cold

Chilly

Shivery

We feel ...

Freezing

Perishing

Frozen stiff

■ After the initial round-up of words, the thesaurus can be consulted to see what other words might be found for the list.

■ 'Glacial' might appeal to some children. 'Polar' might appear on the list.

■ Talk about the 'order of coldness' of these words: Is 'freezing' colder than 'perishing'? There won't necessarily be any agreement on this but this doesn't matter; it is the discussion that is important.

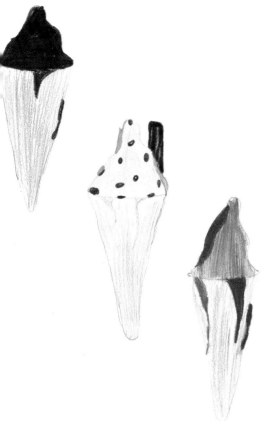

■ These can feature in a 'Now I know what it feels like' poem.

> Now I know what an ice-cream feels like.
> When you burn me with your fiery lips
> My poor white skin just melts away.
> Just wait!
> I'll make you shiver!

D.O.

> Now I know what a football net feels like.
> Freezing cold pitches
> Old cold toes
> Rattling inside boots until the game starts.
> The ball is zooming at me
> When the kick-off starts.
> Nets are cool - well that's what I think!

Adam, Edward, Rory, David

A 'getting colder' poem is a possibility here:
> I'm chilly,
> I feel like butter in the fridge,
> Or a rock out in the garden.

> I'm cold,
> My fingers are falling off,
> My face is going blue.

> I'm freezing
> I'm in the freezer,
> I'm a block of ice ...

The poem might then come indoors and warm up again!

■ Another pattern might describe the weather getting steadily colder through the week, or though the hours of the day.
  - On Monday ...
  - On Tuesday ...
■ The thesaurus can also help us with a list of cold *things and places*, and this list can be extended by the children.
  - Inside a fridge
  - Snow
  - Ice cube
  - Ice-cream
  - The North Pole
  - A winter garden

Other ideas might be:
  - *Now I know what a snowman feels like when the sun comes out*
  - *Now I know what a fire feels like when the fire brigade turn on their hoses ...*
■ *'Cold' is given here as an example of 'Thesaurus Game' possibilities.*
■ *There are many words that make a good starting point and for older children more abstract ideas such as 'Fear' and 'Anger' work well.*
■ *It is essential that the initial word is based in some way on a real experience.*

ASSOCIATIONS

- In the 'Thesaurus Game' we looked for a range of words associated with a particular idea.
- 'Associations' takes the opposite angle.

We are looking here at the various associations that have 'attached' themselves to words. 'Cold' for example is connected with temperature, but the word has other associations; unemotional, unsympathetic, for instance.

Here is the result of a free association game based on the word 'hands'.

'Good' or 'happy' Associations	'Bad' or 'sad' Associations
holding	waving goodbye
giving	grabbing
stroking	claws
patting heads	sharp nails
shaking hands	strangle
clapping	hit
prayers	stealing
holding hands	tearing with bare hands
clean	dirty

The lists created from the 'Association Game' can be used as the basis of some interesting poems incorporating various aspects and associations of the original idea.

Other good Association Game starters:
- Parents
- Eyes
- School
- Animals
- Heat
- Mouths.

Hands

Hands are nice and giving,
stroking and patting
Hands are ... hands are.

Hands are good at writing,
drawing and clapping
Hands are ... hands are.

Hands are clever at throwing
and clicking
Hands are ... hands are.

Hands are on a clock, ticking,
Hands are ... hands are.

Hands are for punching,
grabbing and slapping,
Hands are, hands are.

Hands are for picking,
stealing and scraping,
Hands are, hands are.

Oliver and Stewart

I am a nasty hand
My hobby is punching everybody
The thing I like best is scratching
I can't help it, I'm always breaking things,
And stealing.
Nobody likes me, I don't know why.
I don't care.

Caroline and Faye

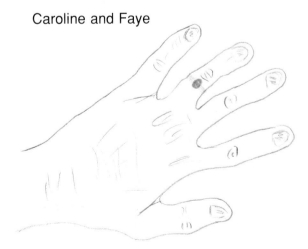

Another approach to the idea of associations is to use the model of a tree. The trunk is a starter idea, and associations spread out like branches. The tree model can be used as a brainstorming device. Give out photocopies of a blank tree for the class to fill in with words and phrases.

■ *Large versions can be made, using colour or collage and look good as display work.*

Starters: words   43

WONDERFUL VERBS . . . AND NOUNS

Verbs are at the heart of poetry. They are very powerful words - use with care! Nouns may seem the most ordinary words, but extraordinary poems can be produced!

The class will enjoy this poem by James Reeves: a super example of the use of strong verbs.

Start with a Thesaurus Game to fill in gaps in dramatic sentences such as these:
- The giant .... through the forest
- The snake .... over the rocks
- The eagle .... over the hills.

■ Try and collect an interesting verb from as many children as possible.
■ Inevitably conventional, cliched ones (marched/slithered/soared) will be offered first; this is a necessary 'clearing the decks' exercise.
■ Discourage auxiliary verbs: 'The Giant was stalking' is weaker than 'The Giant stalked'. The verbs offered can then be given back to the class.

Giant Thunder

Giant Thunder, striding home,
Wonders if his supper's done.

'Hag wife, hag wife, bring me my bones!'
'They are not done,' the old hag moans.

'Not done? Not done?' the giant roars
And heaves his old wife out of doors.

Cries he, 'I'll have them, cooked or not!'
But overturns the cooking pot.

He flings the burning coals about;
See how the lightning flashes out!

Upon the gale the old hag rides,
The cloudy moon for terror hides.

All the world with thunder quakes;
Forest shudders, mountain shakes;
From the cloud the rainstorm breaks;
Village ponds are turned to lakes;
Every living creature wakes.

Hungry Giant, lie you still!
Stamp no more from hill to hill -
Tomorrow you shall have your fill.

James Reeves

Individually or in groups they can select from the list to tell the story of the giant, or the snake; or perhaps the story of a battle between two very different enemies, using two sets of verbs.

The dinosaur squelched through the swamp,
Then crashed and thumped through the trees.

His enemy, the robot, clicked and creaked from his hiding place.

Rumble! Bump! Crunch!

Rattle! Clank clank!
Chuggachugga ... spark ... fizz.

Guess who won?

Group poem

The idea is to create a short name for something that doesn't actually mention the proper word. These poems using nouns are called Kennings.

■ *Here are some suggestions for names for* **Water**, *devised by class 2 at William Penn Primary School, Sussex:*

- *An animal-refresher*
- *A ship-holder*
- *A fish-breather*
- *A fire-drowner*
- *A rock-rusher*
- *A river-runner*
- *A tap-zoomer*
- *A rain-holder*
- *A snow-melter*
- *A water-mill pusher*
- *A photo-finisher*
- *A plant-feeder*
- *A hose-splasher*
- *A car-washer*
- *A wave-crasher*
- *A food-processor*
- *A grass-grower*
- *A glasses-rinser*
- *A loo-flusher*
- *A sky-dropper*
- *An egg-boiler*
- *A perfume sprayer*
- *A fountain-player*
- *A jelly-maker*
- *A cube-creator*
- *A radiator-dasher*
- *A body-cooler*
- *A bike-sparkler*
- *A brush-cleaner*
- *A wave-mover*
- *A food-cooker.*

■ *The idea of Kennings can be extended to neologisms (made up words) of all sorts. Read 'Jabberwocky' then try making up words.*

■ *Some ideas might be:*
- *A word that means the sound of ...*
- *A word that explains how you feel when ...*
- *A word that describes the way a ... moves.*

From 'Jabberwocky'

'Twas brillig, and the slithy toves
Did gyre and gimble in the wabe;
All mimsy were the borogroves,
And the mome raths outgrabe.

'Beware the Jabberwock, my son!
The jaws that bite, the claws that catch!
Beware the Jubjub bird and shun
The frumious Bandersnatch!'

Lewis Carroll

I AND YOU

● Children should be encouraged to think about when it is appropriate to use the first person, I, and the third person he, she, it.

I of course is used for writing about real experiences and opinions, but there are other possibilities suggested below. There are a number of interesting possibilities for using the second person, in which the writer directly addresses a person or object and I have included a number of these. Apart from the interesting writing that can be produced, this work extends children's knowledge about how language works in an enjoyable and practical way. Information on matters such as identifying parts of speech, on tense and person, is useful and important but if presented through dry exercise it is immediately forgettable.

I can be used for mask poems in which the poet takes on the persona of another person, an animal, or even an inanimate object - see 'Now I know what it feels like' poems on page 41.

Such poems are attractively presented by being written on masks, or mounted with masks.

Children can wear the masks to perform their poems for an assembled group.

Mask poems lead naturally on to riddle writing (see page 52) in which the audience have to guess what the poet is.

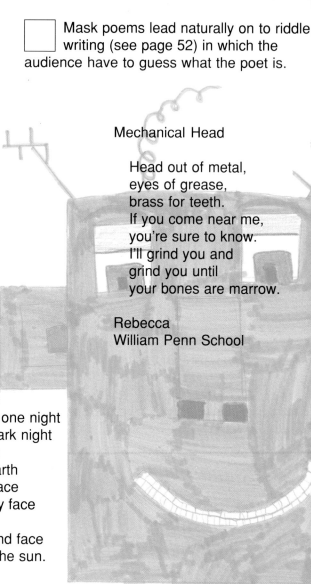

Mechanical Head

Head out of metal,
eyes of grease,
brass for teeth.
If you come near me,
you're sure to know.
I'll grind you and
grind you until
your bones are marrow.

Rebecca
William Penn School

I'm the Grin

I'm the grin
I came out one night
one very dark night
I'm the grin
I grin on earth
I grin in space
I grin on my face

My big round face
gleams in the sun.

Sarah Beale
William Penn School

■ Another possibility is to become an abstrac idea or emotion: I am anger ...

The ode is, of course, a tradition in classic English poetry, and there are many famous ones.

Ode to the West Wind

> O wild West Wind, thou breath of Autumn's being,
> Thou, driven from whose unseen presence the leaves dead
> Are driven, like ghosts from an enchanter fleeing ...

Shelley

Ode to Autumn

> Season of mists and mellow fruitfulness,
> Close bosom-friend of the maturing sun;

Keats

It is difficult for poets to get away with the archaic 'thee' and 'thou' these days, of course!

Using 'you' offers a range of possibilities

Odes. These can describe a friend, enemy, creature, or even an object using 'you'.

I hate you.
You have big green warts on your nose,
Your hair is like greasy parcel string ...

Oh, dear shoe,
Whatever would I do
If I didn't have you?

Giving instructions. Grammatically, this involves using the imperative: I sometimes call these Imperative Poems.

How to pass your driving test - perhaps

> *Drive too fast and run people over,*
> *That's the way to pass your test!*
>
> *Indicate right and turn to the left,*
> *Only go over lights when they are red,*
> *That's the way to pass your test!*
>
> *Shout and flash your lights at other drivers,*
> *Go the wrong way up dual carriageways,*
> *Take both hands off the wheel to light a cigarette,*
> *That's the way the pass the test!*

Other possibilities are spells, recipes, comic or gruesome instructions for repairing cars or carrying out a surgical operation ... and so on!

■ *Curses. This can be entertaining if not taken seriously.*
> - *A curse on the person who took my computer game ...*
> - *May you be electrocuted when you switch it on,*
> - *May your ears light up and your teeth fall out ...*

COMPARISONS - THE IMAGINATIVE LEAP

- Children vary enormously in their readiness to make the imaginative leap from the *real world* to the world of the *imagination.*

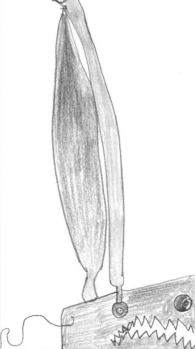

Young children do have a gift for thinking in metaphor, and creating a fantasy world of their own, the world of the imagination, in which prosaic vacuum cleaners can become voracious creatures! See page 56.

Learning the terms 'metaphor' and 'simile' and the distinction between them is not particularly helpful at this stage - this can come later.

The strong wind's dark voice is an invisible town crier ...

Openers. Young children enjoy talking about how their imaginations work during the night. The following poem can stimulate discussion. Ask the class how many of them play the games described; talk about other games they play, and why they think 'imagination' works so powerfully at night.

Night Fright

You know those things that terrify at night;
Secretly I know that they're not true
And yet I love to give myself a fright.

The bathroom game; you never know what might
Come after you when you've just flushed the loo;
That's just one thing that terrifies at night.

You hear a car behind you, see its lights,
You run and run in fear of what they'll do;
Home safe! I love to give myself a fright.

Some teachers may question whether the use of frightening, horrible images like these justified, and obviously if there are doubts as to the suitability of this approach with individual children it should be avoided. In my experience, however, discussion of such fears is helpful rather than the reverse.

What could it be? games. Make a collection of sound effects on tape. Start with genuine guesses, then move to more imaginative possibilities. Extend the ideas into stories and poems.

Animal Dreams. What do animals dream of? What might the wind, sun or moon dream of? What might a car dream of?

The lamp-post game. Air's poison by that light,
You hold your breath until you're safely through;
Another thing that terrifies at night.

The beasts that come when you've switched out the light
Who'll feast off all uncovered bits of you;
It seems I love to give myself a fright.

And cracks in pavements, shadow shapes that bite -
In darkness there is always something new,
Some awful thing to terrify at night.
How strange we love to give ourselves such fright.

.O.

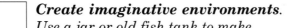

Create imaginative environments.
Use a jar or old fish tank to make underwater pebble gardens, or use chemicals to make 'chemical gardens'.
■ *Tissue box worlds.* With thanks to Moira Andrew whose idea it was.

Create a scene inside a tissue box: this can be a strange planet, a dinosaur world, an undersea world.

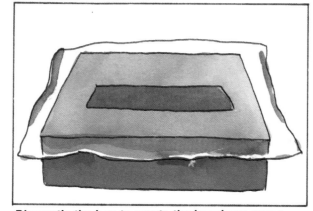

Dismantle the box to create the imaginary scene, then cover the hole in the top, and, if required, the 'back wall' with coloured cellophane.

Look through the spy hole at the new world created.

Use a torch to vary the lighting effects.

Undersea world

In my undersea world,
A giant octopus dreams of juicy fish;
Grey sharks slice invisible cakes.
Deep in a dark cave,
An unknown monster
Lurks ...

William

- **The structure of Ezras.**
  The first line is the real, observed world, (although some children might pick up the 'hidden' metaphor in 'apparition').
  The second line exists in the world of the imagination only.

MATCHBOX POEMS OR 'EZRAS'

This idea is based on the famous Ezra Pound poem:

In the Station of the Metro

The apparition of those faces in the crowd;
Petals on a wet, black bough.

Stage 1: provide the class with a first line from the 'real' world.

Do not offer a choice at this stage; we want the class to concentrate on thinking through the comparisons rather than on choosing their subject. Their task is then to invent the second line. Children should work in pairs for this.

Possible 'first lines'.
- The sound of the wind in the night.
- An old, leafless tree. Try and make it a specific tree visible from the classroom.
- The dark shadow on the wall.
- The flames of the bonfire.
- The tall block of flats.
- Thick fog on the road.
- Lamp-posts in the city street.

Stage 2: ask each child to think of a first line, in the way that you did; something from the real world. The idea is then that partners exchange first lines and come up with a second line for their partner's real world idea.

Displaying the matchbox poems.
Children will enjoy drawing the picture in which lamp-posts really do turn into flamingoes:

Lamp-posts in the high street;
Bright flamingoes by the river.

Matchbox poems by Laura

Hot, steaming bubble baths;
Big, frothy witch's cauldrons.

Cats miowing to be let in;
A wheel that needs to be oiled.

Fluttering butterflies;
The beating of hearts.

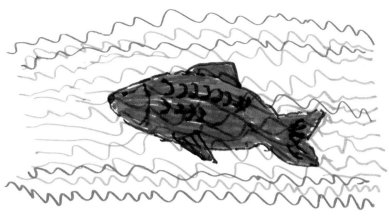

■ Extend this idea by building up a series of matchbox poems into a poem describing a particular place - a city street, a forest, the school.

■ **Comparison lists.** Back to lists, and to the chalkboard! The idea here is to see how many ideas can come from one 'real world' starter. Try and obtain an idea from everyone in the class. This will ensure that any stale, dull ideas are used up to start with, and the children will really have to stretch to think of new ones.

The sound of the wind in the night is like ...

A howling werewolf on a hill
An unhappy ghost looking for its treasure
The sea breaking on the rocks
A kettle boiling only there's no one to make the tea
A steam train roaring through a station
Frightened people whistling to cheer themselves up
A thousand snakes trying to get in
The hiss of a safe-breaker's blow-torch.

Now get rid of the 'like'

The wind in the night is ...

■ The various ideas can then be patterned, in this case perhaps in order of loudness as the storm gets more and more violent.
This poem is ideal for choral speaking and performance.
More visual things, such as goldfish, lend themselves to attractive display.

Goldfish

The goldfish in the pond are like

Pound coins in a wishing well
Ingots from a sunken pirate ship
Copper pipes in a junk yard
Amber traffic lights in the rain
Segments of an orange fallen on the grass
Glowing carrots swimming in salad dressing
Nigel Mansel in his gold Ferrari
Diving and crashing aeroplanes
Bullets shot out of a gun
Scales of a forlorn dragon shed with sorrow
Fireballs speeding through the sky on a hot day
Coppery bronze arrows shooting at the reeds.

The writer has now moved from simile to metaphor, but again there is no need to use the terms. Children are capable of using poetic devices without slavishly learning their names. In fact, this kind of restriction of the writer's subject matter can often be more of a stimulus than the usual 'free' writing.

RIDDLING

- Riddles start with word games, and can develop into poems of considerable subtlety.
- Their link with poetry is the use of metaphor and simile.
- With riddles, the object is for the reader or listener to guess what the 'real world' idea is.

There is a tradition of riddles - and riddling power - that goes back many centuries. The Anglo-Saxons were enthusiastic riddlers. This is a well-known one:

When I walk the earth, make tracks upon the water
or keep close to houses, silent is my clothing,
clothing that lifts me above roof tops,
or tosses me into the high heavens
where the powerful cloud-wind carries me on
over towns and countries;
my limbs throb out sound, thrilling strokes
of deep-sighing song,
I sail alone
Over field and flood,
resting no-where. My name is ...

The answer is, of course, a swan.

Ask your class if they can solve the riddle of the Sphinx:

What goes on four legs in the morning,
Two legs in the afternoon,
And three legs in the evening?

The answer, of course, is Man - he crawls as a baby, walks upright as an adult, and uses a stick in his old age.

Runes. Anglo-Saxon riddles were ofte written using runes. These are useful for the presentation of riddles and much fun can be had communicating in them.

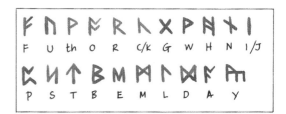

■ **Building riddles.** Riddles describe familia things as if they were something else; something that shares a feature or features with the thing described. Very often these ar written in the first person (see page 46).

What am I?

I have four legs but I cannot walk
My back aches when you are comfortable.

(A chair)

■ A good starter idea, or working with a class is a TV set:

It has buttons, one big eye; and can contain the whole world inside it!

Riddles work well as group work, especially when groups are able to challenge other groups to solve their riddles! The following rules for riddles can be offered to your class:

RULE 1
Do not have a title

RULE 2
Pretend you are the thing you are writing about

RULE 3
Describe something accurately but make it sound strange. "I am a black screen that never runs out" is in fact a chalkboard.

RULE 4
You have to say enough so it can be only one thing. For example if you think of a table and say "I have four legs", this can also be a horse in your listener's mind.

RULE 5
Avoid saying too much. You will write something too easy and it will be no fun to work out!

My first is in ... These riddles have gone out of fashion somewhat, which is a shame as children enjoy compiling them and working them out. Again, start simply.

My first is in CAT but not in DOG,
My second's in SNOW and also in FOG,
My last is in WHY and also in HOW,
My whole is an animal known as a ...

Crackerjokes. *Collect 'question and answer' riddles from the class; these are the sort of riddles commonly found in crackers, thus the invented name! Many are based on puns, or other word play:*
- *What did the beaver say to the tree?*
- *It's been nice gnawing you!*
Others use the imagination a little more:
- *What's green and goes up and down?*
- *A gooseberry in a lift!*

■ *An enjoyable exercise is to ask the class to make their own slips of paper for the inside of crackers; the slip should include a 'crackerjoke' but might also have a 'quiz' type question, or 'fascinating fact' item with an appropriate picture.*

You can feel me,
but you can't touch me
or see me.
I am very strong
　　What am I?

Lucy

I am a black screen
That never runs out
At the end of the day
You can brush my face
away
What am I?

Richard

I am a green ball with a tough, spiny coat.
My heart is full
Of the start of me.

Richard

Like an elephant's head,
I squirt water on the flowers
With my trunk.

Leonie

I let off light
But I am not a light bulb
I melt down
But I am not an ice-cream
I look like a thick white stick
I disappear when I am used
　　What am I?

Lucy

■ Answers: wind, chalkboard, conker, watering-can, candle.

OBJECTS

- The important thing is that the objects need to be safe to handle, relatively unbreakable, and interesting in terms of the senses.

For this poem - making activity, you will need to acquire a range of interesting and evocative objects; one for each group.

Start by asking the groups to write down their sense impressions of the object.

Possibilities are:
- stones or pieces of wood with interesting shapes or colours
- plants of various sorts
- other natural objects: fruits, seeds, leaves
- kitchen implements
- small carvings
- 'scientific' items.

Every classroom should have a collection of such objects.

What does it

FEEL like?

TASTE like? (take care!)

LOOK and SMELL like? (colour, shape)

SOUND like? (if you tap it)

Lighthouse poem - a pink candle

In Australia,
On a rainbow,
There is a lighthouse
Where a man lives on the colour pink.
He collects sharp shells from the pink sea
Around a pier.
The shells leave dents in the pink sand.
The man puts the shells round his lighthouse
At night the sea brings all the shells in,
Smashing them against the pier.

Sheena

The story of the gargoyles - an alabaster egg

In the castle moat I found
An old, old egg.
A drop of water fell on me,
I looked up to see
A gargoyle of a pterodactyl.
He was crying.
On a stone were the words:
'Find the head of the basilisk!
It turned me and my egg into stone.
If you shield your eyes,
and show him the egg,
I will be free!'

Lucy and Laura

Now extend the idea of *likeness* with these questions:
- If you had ever seen anything like this before, what might you guess about it?
- What other things does it remind you of? Encourage children to come up with as many ideas as possible.

At this point, other, even more imaginative questions are a possibility:
- What do you think the object dreams about?
- What questions would you like to ask the object?
- What might the answers be?
- What sort of person would this object make?

And so on.
The assembled ideas and notes can then be worked up into poems.

An extension of these activities would be to ask the groups to work on the same object, one after the other, but without consulting with other groups. If you are lucky, there will be a range of different ideas, which can be used to make an unusual display with the original object at the centre.

STRETCHING

Once children have confidence in working with metaphor and simile they can be encouraged to explore and extend their initial idea, perhaps a 'matchbox poem', into a longer piece.

This process can take place initially as a class poem. Start by finding existing extended metaphor poems, such as this one.

The sea is a hungry dog,
Giant and grey.
He rolls on the beach all day.
With his clashing teeth and shaggy jaws
Hour upon hour he gnaws
The rumbling, tumbling, stones,
And 'Bones, bones, bones!'
The giant sea-dog moans,
Licking his greasy paws.

And when the night wind roars
And the moon rocks in the stormy cloud,
He bounds to his feet and snuffs and sniffs,
Shaking his wet sides over the cliffs,
And howls and hollos long and loud.

But on quiet days of May or June,
When even the grasses on the dune
Play no more their reedy tune,
With his head between his paws
He lies on the sandy shores,
So quiet, so quiet, he scarcely snores.

James Reeves

Once children have their imaginative idea, ask them to tell the story. Oliver saw a chain-saw as a monster: he was asked to tell the story of the monster.

The chainsaw

A roaring monster
With a spinning tail,
Bits of wood like sparks of electricity fly viciously from
Its victims,
Greedily eating away
Finishing its meal it starts to hum.
I wonder if it has to brush its teeth?

Oliver

For Matthew and Stewart, the vacuum cleaner becomes a bird of prey ...

A vacuum cleaner

Press the button
It flies
Gathering speed
Landing on a perch
Looking around dangerously
Catching its victims
With strong noisy
Gulps
Nothing
Remains.

Matthew and Stewart

This poem started off with the idea of scuttling insects looking like footballers rushing round a pitch. Mark and Michael extended it by telling the story of the match.

Creepy-Crawly Acorn Cup Final

Today's the day!
Insects squashed together
Thrilled and excited
Here to see the match of the year!
Two teams, nervous, ready for the game,
West Wormery,
Wiggly, thin and skilful.
Snails United,
Slow but brilliant.
On to the pitch the two teams jog
Excited and proud.
The ref, Beetle Bug-Bite, tosses a carrot top.
Snails win.
Off they go!

Running up the left wing flies Slimey Sid.
The crowd roars.
The ball crosses over to Sammy Shell.
Into the goal area it goes,
The crowd is wild.
The scarves on the end of their antennae wave in the wind.
Slippery Simon backflips the ball,
Into the net it goes.
IT'S A GOAL!
The atmosphere is electric.
Back to the centre.
Wally Wallace passes to Willy Wigglesworth

A chip from Walter Wimble send it back to Wally Wallace.
He volleys it from outside the penalty area.
A GOAL to West Wormery.
Just in time.
Beetle Bug-Bite blows his whistle.
IT'S ALL OVER.
ONE-ALL.
Back they must all come again,
To fight for the acorn cup another day!

Mark and Michael

SHAPE POEMS

- Concrete poetry, or shape poems, are:
  - visually appealing
  - eccentric
  - able to extend and challenge children's perception of what poems are.

The basic principle is that the pattern the poem makes on the page represents, in some way, what the subject of the poem is. Possibilities are endless; the shape poems on this page show some of the possibilities.

Adults find the eccentricity of shape poems needs some getting used to; children usually see the logic of them immediately.

Before starting:
  - offer lots of examples before children attempt their own
  - discuss with them why the poems are odd, yet successful.

Afterwards:
  - try performance of any if possible
  - explore any sounds created through taping and groupwork.

Concrete poems can be as big, small, colourful as the children like.

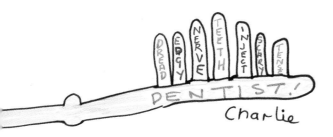

DREAD EDGY NERVE TEETH INJECT SCARY TENSE

PENTIST!

Charlie

'One letter poems' make an unusual variant.

children wait
expertly then
whizz round and
round and round
round and land and BUMP!

Craig

B B B B B B B B

HIVE

T T T T T T T

POT OF TEA

Q Q Q Q Q

BUS STOP

REPETITION

- Rhythm, rhyme, alliteration, stanza patterns, are all examples of repetition in poetry.
- Another is the use of a refrain, a repeating line or stanza in a poem.

Songs such as 'The Drunken Sailor' have a refrain which those new to the song can soon pick up, enabling them to join in. Refrains are an important part of the oral tradition. They provide a structure for writing, appeal to young children who enjoy repetition, and offer a range of possibilities for performance.

That horrible feeling when you wake
up in the middle of the night
and it's cold and dark
and you need
to go to
the loo ...

With the class, devise a rhyming couplet to act as a refrain. One possibility is a poem about the members of the group or class:

What are we like? well, come and see,
The peculiar folk who are found in class 3!

Each member can then write a short poem about themselves: these can be linked together by the refrain lines.

■ **Other possibilities.**
- Events on a journey, with the sound of the bus/car/train featuring in the refrain.
- A spell, with a 'mixing' refrain - borrow the refrain from the witches' song in Macbeth.
- A zoo or wildlife poem - animal noises make a good refrain.
- A more sophisticated pattern is to invent two different, alternating refrains. These poems make very attractive performance pieces.

What do you do,
What do you do,
When it's dark
And you need
To go to the loo?

It's warm and snug
As you lie in your bed,
And you think about going
To sleep instead,
But deep in your head,
A voice keeps saying,

It has been suggested throughout this book that the use of a repeated line can turn simple lists into poems for performance (page 34). Poems such as 'That Horrible Feeling ...' take this a stage further.

Come on! Get up!
You know, you know,
You can't go to sleep
You've got to go!

So

What do you do,
What do you do,
When it's dark
And you need
To go to the loo?

You think
I'm sure that I
Don't need to go!
I'm warm and I'm sleepy
The bathroom at night
Is cold and creepy
I'll curl up in bed,
You never know,
That feeling might just go away ...

But you hear that voice say...
Come on! Get up!
You know, you know,
You can't go to sleep.
You've got to go!

So

What do you do,
What do you do,
When it's dark
And you need
To go to the loo?

You put out a toe
You put out a foot
You put out a leg
It's cold! and so
You find your dressing gown
You threw on the floor

Wrap it round you
Open the door

And as fast as you can

You go.

David Orme

Other possibilities including repetition include:
- *the question and answer poem*
- *repeating lines throughout a poem.*

Both ideas are used in 'Lord Randall', a hypnotically powerful ballad of mystery and murder:

'O where hae ye been, Lord Randall my son?
O where hae ye been, my handsome young man?'
'I hae been to the wild wood; mother, make my bed soon,
For I'm weary wi' hunting, and fain would lie down.'

'Where gat ye your dinner, Lord Randall, my son?
Where gat ye your dinner, my handsome young man?'
'I dined wi' my true love; mother make my bed soon,
For I'm weary wi' hunting, and fain would lie down!'

- **It is important for children to experiment with syllables and not just because knowledge of them is necessary for advanced work on poetic theory!**

COUNTING SYLLABLES

Work on syllable counting brings enormous benefits to listening and speaking skills. It can also lead on to concepts of rhythm. (See page 74)

Definitions of syllables are tricky and confusing, so start with a game.

Teacher: A cat has one, a rabbit has two, what animal has three?

Class: (blank faces!)

Teacher: Well, have a guess; you all know plenty of animals!

Class: Dog?

Teacher: No! *(and so on until someone chooses a three syllable animal such as elephant or kangaroo.)*

Teacher: Yes!

At this point the penny will drop for some of the more alert members of the class. If not, the teacher repeats the names of the animals one syllable at a time. The word syllable can then be introduced if the class do not know it. The definition 'sound chunk' is unscientific but descriptive.

Start with their own names. Ask them to work out how many 'sound chunks' are in their own name and how it is different from a partner's, e.g. Nee - deep Pa - tel is very different in both syllable pattern and therefore rhythm, to Al - ex - an - der Bar- ker.
■ The class will now enjoy finding animals with four, five six and more syllables ...
 - Alligator
 - Hippopotamus
 - Tyrannosaurus Rex
 - Lesser Spotted Woodpecker.

■ **Diamond poems.** These poems start reducing the syllable count once a certain point is reached. They are a more difficult challenge than growing poems as ingenuity is required to reach a satisfying conclusion. An extra degree of sophistication can be added by writing about something that expands and then contracts, or goes up and then down.

Kite
up
it flies.
Higher and
higher, rising
all the time. The wind
drops. Gradually it falls
down and down, lower
and lower it
hits the ground,
bounces ...
dies ...

Richard

gum
sticky
lovely gum
strawberry pink
puff, blow, here we go
scrumdiddly umptious
oh! the lovely taste
blueberries blue
cola brown
yum yum
POP!

Ruth

■ **Growing poems.** These poems have one syllable in the first line, two in the second, three in the third, and so on, as long as you wish to make them! Lead in by offering a four line growing poem and ask the class to make up the next line. They will soon pick up the rule and be ready to write their own growing poems.

Once,
I saw
A tiger
eating ice-cream ...

Simple syllabics. *Look at ballads and talk about the syllable pattern - usually 8, 6, 8, 6. Beating these out to make the music is a fun way of doing this. Don't forget our old friend the limerick either - 8, 8, 5, 5, 8.*

■ *Suggest that children try their own syllable poems; then talk about which patterns are the most successful. They could name the forms after themselves to make them more special.*

SYLLABIC POEMS

- Haiku and cinquain are both popular in schools.
- These pages seek to give the teacher new approaches to them.
- Some will argue that the point of a Haiku isn't the pattern, but the content; a sudden moment of awareness. The best Japanese Haiku have this quality of suddenly seeing the world in a fresh light. In any case, it is very difficult to retain the pattern when a poem is translated.

The Haiku is a short formal Japanese poem. Its English version is a three line poem, with a 5-7-5 syllable pattern.

> In the morning sun
> Grass is cold, damp, and crunchy
> Then out comes the sun.

Craig

The Cinquain, sometimes thought of as Japanese in origin, was actually devised by an American poet, Adelaide Crapsey. It provides more of a challenge than Haiku and has a more interesting pattern of 2, 4, 6, 8, and 2 syllable lines.

Triad

> These be
> Three silent things:
> The falling snow ... the hour
> Before the dawn ... the mouth of one
> Just dead.

Adelaide Crapsey

Writing them is popular in schools; why is this?

✔ They produce a short, polished, finished product ensuring a successful outcome. They can be produced without lengthy labour. Children find two aspects of writing difficult: getting started and knowing when to stop. Fixed patterns like this solve the latter problem.

✔ The discipline in working to a fixed number of syllables is in itself valuable. The difficulty of it provides a puzzle element that children enjoy, and the search for synonyms and the rearrangement of lines to produce the right number of syllables extends vocabulary and writing skills. Restriction can become a form of liberation.

Teachers will need to decide for themselves to what extent they should insist that the pattern is adhered to. Certainly, in a batch of Haiku children should try and produce at least one according to the rules.

Always keep in mind the words of David McCord:

> Syllable writing,
> Counting out your seventeen,
> Doesn't produce poem.

> Good Haiku need thought:
> One simple statement followed
> By poet's comment.

> The town dump is white
> With seagulls, like butterflies
> Over a garden.

Children's Games. Use the picture of this name by Pieter Brueghel the Elder. Children love looking at it to see what is going on. Every square inch is filled with activity. Get the children to choose one of the groups of children to write their Haiku about. This not only provides a good starting point for writing but can also provide an effective piece of display.

Onward go the blind.
Slowly as they walk.
All is a shadow.

Clip, clop, boys on stilts.
Snicker-snacker, here they come -
Towering giants!

Hop on the child's train
It won't take you very far -
Running in a line.

Riding a barrel
Galloping down rolling streets
But getting nowhere.

There are boys banging,
Scuffing and hitting wood
Hitting sticks on bricks.

■ **The Cinquain** starts like a growing poem, but snaps back like an elastic band at the end. Finding a satisfactory two syllable conclusion is a challenge, to which 'the end' should be firmly ruled out as unworthy! Suggest that children do not start the poem at the beginning, and work through to the end. This will make the ending very difficult.

■ Short poems such as these present a single idea, or experience, with economy and simplicity, and the form presents a 'prop' for children who find getting started difficult. Here are some cinquains from Lucy's sequence, 'The Seasons'.

February

    Rainy
    Woolly jumper
    Put my umbrella up
    February freezes the lakes
    Ice ponds.

July

    School's out
    Nothing to do
    The holidays are here
    The apricots are fresh and ripe
    Heaven!

September

    Apples
    Back to school now
    Sportsmen now aim their guns
    Towards wild pheasants in the grass.

THE IMAGINATIVE LEAP - AGAIN

- **The point of such very short poems like Haiku and Cinquain was the expression of a sudden awareness of an aspect of the world seen in a new light.**

Although he did not write in these fixed forms, the American poet Charles Reznikoff saw sudden beauty in unlikely surroundings and his poems have the same impact as the best Japanese Haiku:

About an excavation

    About an excavation
    a flock of bright red lanterns
    has settled.

If the poetry work we do can sensitise children to these experiences we will have achieved something of enormous value.

Haiku and cinquain may present the single powerful image without recourse to overt metaphor as in the lanterns turning into birds. There is usually, however, some implied metaphor or comparison in even the simplest poem.

    Girls planting paddy
    Only their song
    Free of the mud.

Konishi Raizan (Tr. Bownas and Thwaite)

Here, the purity of the singing is in sharp contrast to the mud.

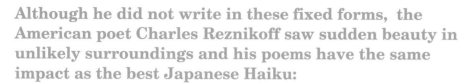

Haikus of contrast. It is useful, when working on Haiku, to have an end in view that goes beyond merely trying to make the pattern work.

The idea of 'beauty in unlikely surroundings' has value far beyond its merits as a language exercise.

Group Haiku.

    Green glass on the beach,
    Glistening in the morning sun;
    Broken emeralds.

    Dustcarts revving up;
    Dirty yellow erasers
    Smudging out rubbish.

Our local tip

    Our local tip:
    An enormous treasure chest,
    Old cars like new homes.

Lucy

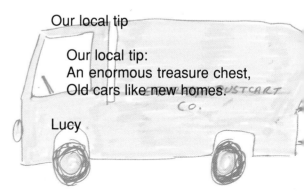

Two Simile cinquains . This Adelaide Crapsey cinquain provides a useful model for linking the work on the imaginative leap with that on patterning.

November night

Listen ...
With faint, dry sound,
Like steps of passing ghosts,
The leaves, frost-crisped, break from the trees
And fall.

The strength of this poem is in the simile (a direct comparison using 'as' or 'like') in the third line. Beginning the third line with 'like' is a useful model for children.

Splish, splash,
Down comes the rain;
Like a dog drooling after
A run with its owner because
It's wet.

James Baggott

■ The cinquain is more difficult to structure than the Haiku. In particular, the last line causes a problem - children suddenly discover they have only 2 syllables in which to finish the poem. These ideas might be useful:
- Start off with the central image
  Spiders = brooms
  and then put this in the middle of the poem - use 'like' if it helps.
- Think of a strong first line and last line.
- Build out from the image to join the poem together.
- Draft and redraft!

The sky
Bewitching blue
Like water; crystal clear,
A rusty red as the day turns
To night.

Natalie Sibbald

Spiders
Climbing up webs
Like broomsticks bristles
Sweeping across the kitchen floor
Creepy

James

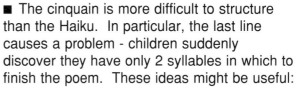

I never saw an ugly thing in my life: for let the form of an object be what it may - light, shade, and perspective will always be beautiful.

John Constable.

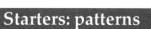

FREE VERSE

- Free verse is sometimes regarded as poetry without rhyme, rhythm, or any of the other poetic devices that give poetry its form. This view is inaccurate.

The point about free verse is that it follows no predetermined pattern but generates a unique one of its own, using all the resources that the poet has.

A free verse poem may be just as tightly structured as any Shakespearean sonnet. One of the great modern masters of free verse is e.e.cummings:

here's a little mouse) and

here's a little mouse) and
what does he think about, i
wonder as over this
floor (quietly with

bright eyes) drifts (nobody
can tell because
Nobody knows, or why
jerks Here &, here,
gr(oo)ving the room's Silence) this like
a littlest
poem a
(with wee ears and see?

tail frisks)
      (gonE)

"mouse",
      We are not the same you and

i, since here's a little he
or is
it It
?   (or was something we saw in the mirror)?

therefore we'll kiss; for maybe
what was Disappeared
into ourselves
who   (look)   ,startled

e.e. cummings

Free verse is not an 'easy option', and children are more comfortable with predetermined patterns to provide a framework for their writing.

Shape poems (page 58) are a good way into the idea that poems can generate their own patterns; the work on structured narratives (page 80) takes this much further.

■ 'Chopped up prose'. A familiar calumny on modern poetry is that it is merely 'chopped up prose'. In fact, some interesting poetry can be created by literally chopping up prose with scissors. Collage poems using old newspapers are an interesting exercise with older children. The point of the 'chopped up prose' criticism is, of course, that chopping is a random process. Collage poems are not random; they rely for their effect on the usual poetic mix of patterning and juxtaposed contrasting ideas. The poet will be looking for these things in the collage poem under construction.

Lineation. A more measured criticism of free verse is that often little thought is given to lineation - determining when one line should end and another begin. Lineation is a major concern in the work on structured narratives (page 80). An interesting exercise for children is to provide them with poems written out continuously, and ask them to divide them up into lines in groups discussing why they chose the places they did. This can be particularly effective if the continuous poems are handed out in one long strip, along with scissors and glue, so that the groups will literally cut them up and arrange them on the page.

■ Start with a poem with a regular pattern, where the lineation is obvious:

> One two three father caught a flea he put it in a teapot to make a cup of tea

(even here there are alternative patterns; is

> One
> Two
> Three
> Father caught a
> Flea

a possibility?)

Then offer a non-rhymed or lightly rhymed poem written out in the same way. The object is not to re-create the original, necessarily, but to get involved in working on lineation in a practical way.

Archy Poems. Don Marquis wrote a whole series of poems about Archy, a literary cockroach. He is a large cockroach and he types his poems by hurling himself against the typewriter keys. Of course, he cannot hold down the shift keys so there are no capital letters or punctuation! He sees things in a new 'streetwise' way and his stories never turn out as you think they should!

aesop revised by archy

> a wolf met a spring
> lamb drinking
> at a stream
> and said to her
> you are the lamb
> that muddied this stream
> all last year
> so that i could not get a clean fresh drink ...

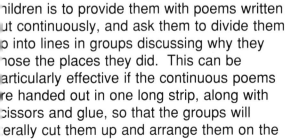

■ *Children could try to make grammatical sense of such poems and talk about the differences between their 'correct' version and the original. They could then invent their own literary animal character who wants to write poems but cannot type. His story could be humorous but will also introduce children to free verse.*

ALLITERATION AND ASSONANCE

- I have defined poetry as 'patterned language' and the most important element of that patterning is sound.

There are a number of technical terms of moderate usefulness to describe this patterning, but attempting to describe the subtle and beautiful sound patterns of the finest poetry by using them is like trying to perform brain surgery with ... an axe! The purpose of all sound patterns in poetry is to make the poem memorable.

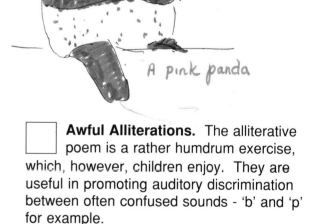

A pink panda

Alliteration is the repetition of initial consonants:
- He clasps the crag with crooked hands ...

Assonance is the repetition of vowel sounds:
- 'sweet dreams ...'

Consonance is the repetition of final consonants:
- 'short and sweet'

Assonance + Consonance or final assonance = rhyme
- 'Sweets are treats'
- 'See me'

Onomatopoeia is a vague term meaning that the sound of the word is similar in some way to the sound of the thing described:
- 'Splash'
- 'Thud'

Moo!

Rattle, Rattle, Shake, Shake

Hubble, Hubble

Awful Alliterations. The alliterative poem is a rather humdrum exercise, which, however, children enjoy. They are useful in promoting auditory discrimination between often confused sounds - 'b' and 'p' for example.
- People prefer patting pink pandas
- Bears bake biscuits in big batches
- Kids kick cola cans across concrete.

Note that sound is the key - hard c and k are interchangeable for this exercise. Note also that the sound can be *inside* a word, as in 'across'. Children can learn to distinguish between hard and soft sounding words and so spelling can be helped. Alliterative poems often turn into number lists - see page 32.

Alliterative pairs. These tell a story in short alliterative lines. These are good poems for pairwork, each member of the pair writing alternate lines.

Football results

Liverpool lost
Darlington drew
Southampton scored
Tottenham tripped over
Fulham failed
West Ham won!

Silly Assonances. Again a useful exercise in auditory discrimination, although it is more difficult to build assonance lines into poems as the assonance struggles hard to turn into rhyme. Short slogans work well:
- 'Don't freeze - feast on green cheese'
- 'The car parks are too far and dark'.

■ **Onomatopoems.** Onomatopoems tell a story through sounds only; visiting the haunted house at night, for example:

Tip tap tip tap tip tap
C R E A K !
Tip tap tip tap tip ...
THUD!
SCREECH!
Tiptaptiptaptiptap
Rattle rattle
CREAK!
Tiptaptiptaptiptaptiptap ...

A variation on this is to ask children to tell the story of an onomatopoem, such as this one:

Suckerslick

Sluckwoozy, sloated suckerslick
Slapperslumping.

SLAT!

Swurgled, mushwacked,
Suckerslick snackered sweetly,

Soggled.

Mango Chutney

NYO-NYO is speaking with your mouth full.

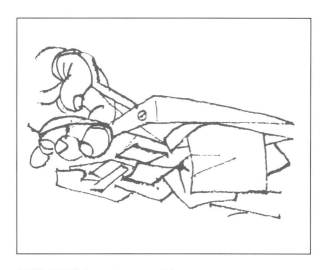

TRIS-TRAS is scissors cutting paper.

TIME FOR RHYME?

- All teachers will be familiar with the dismal rhyming doggerel many children produce when a poem is asked for.
- Rhyme can cause such despair that I have known classrooms where it is banned altogether. Is this a sensible idea?

Children's insistence that poems should rhyme might show a limited appreciation of the possibilities of poetry and might irritate the teacher, but at least it demonstrates that children are aware, however vaguely, that patterning and music are an important element in poetry. Might it be possible to build on this rather than ban it all together?

Rhyme and rhythm are very important in children's early experience of language. Traditionally, they listened to nursery rhymes; now it is more likely to be TV jingles, but the effect is very much the same.

If children listen to a range of poems, well read, they will begin to develop an ear for more subtle musical possibilities.

The question of rhyme can be tackled head on. Children need to know when rhyme is appropriate, and when it's not. They also need guidance on how to use it.

If children have experimented with a range of patterns and forms, and different varieties of rhyme such as half rhyme and eye rhyme, they are unlikely to say 'that's not a poem; it doesn't rhyme!'

I often tell children the following:
- Rhyme makes poetry easy to remember.
- Rhyme can help to make poems funny.

BUT ...

When you write descriptive poems, you need to use just the right word to say what you mean. This is very difficult if you use rhyme. Sometimes, rhyme can make a serious poem funny or silly; not what you intended!

I then illustrate this point with a well-chosen humorous rhyming poem and a descriptive non-rhyming one.

It is misleading, of course, to suggest that descriptive poems never rhyme, or that all rhyming poems are funny.

Rhyming dictionaries. A rhyming dictionary is dangerous if too much reliance is made on it, but children will enjoy using it to build up nonsense poems based on a single rhyme.

Here is the start of a poem based on the Edward Lear favourite, The Akond Of Swat, that provides an entertaining model.

The Akond of Crewe

> When he's woken at night by cats,
> does he chuck a brick or a
>   SHOE
> The Akond of Crewe?

> Does he wear worn-out clothes,
> or does his wife make him buy
>   NEW
> The Akond of Crewe?

> Does he always tell lies,
> Or is every word
>   TRUE,
> The Akond of Crewe?

Here is the start of the original:

The Akond of Swat

> Who or why, or which, or what,
> Is the Akond of SWAT?

> Is he tall or short, or dark or fair?
> Does he sit on a stool or a sofa or a chair,
> or SQUAT,
> The Akond of Swat?

Edward Lear

Getting rid of couplets. Children generally assume that rhymes work in uplets:

rom The Owl-critic

With some sawdust or bark
I could stuff in the dark
an owl better than that
I could make an old hat
Look more like an owl
That that horrid fowl,
Stuck up there so stiff like a side of coarse leather.
In fact, about him there's not one natural feather.

ames Thomas Fields

It is very difficult to write successfully in this way; lots of rhymes are required, and it is difficult to avoid the 'thud' at the end of the couplet. If children are working on rhyme, suggest that they rhyme alternate lines, starting with the second:

From Little Billee

> There were three sailors of Bristol city
> Who took a boat and went to sea.
> But first with beef and captain's biscuits
> And pickled pork they loaded she.

William Makepeace Thackeray

This naturally leads on to ballad writing - see the section on narratives on page 76. Both of these extracts demonstrate one of the problems rhymsters have to face - a regular rhyming pattern demands a regular rhythm.

RHYTHMS AND RAPS

A child's response is subliminal and cannot be taught by rote; it comes through regular listening and experimenting with language, although some of it is built-in. In particular, it comes through performance. The message again, is that poetry cannot be left just as a reading/writing activity.

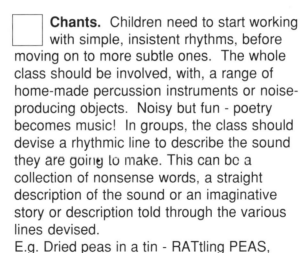

- Poetry needs music and rhythm is a vital component. This does not have to be rumpty-tum!
- Good free verse may seem rhythmless, but there is always a sense of tension, of 'rightness' in the language so that the pattern of sound echoes the sense.
- The iambic metre is at the heart of English poetry and iambics mirror the patterns of ordinary speech.
- Working with iambics can give children a real feel for rhythms.
- Our ultimate aim is that children should recognise and respond to stress and cadence in language.

Chants. Children need to start working with simple, insistent rhythms, before moving on to more subtle ones. The whole class should be involved, with, a range of home-made percussion instruments or noise-producing objects. Noisy but fun - poetry becomes music! In groups, the class should devise a rhythmic line to describe the sound they are going to make. This can be a collection of nonsense words, a straight description of the sound or an imaginative story or description told through the various lines devised.

E.g. Dried peas in a tin - RATtling PEAS, RATling PEAS ...

or, more imaginatively, Pencils tapping radiators could be
PIRates BONES, ROLling in the SEA
Something suitably coin-like could be - PIEces of EIGHT!

Some lines should be short, some long. When the various components of the chant are ready, a performance should be orchestrated. One possibility is to perform the chants individually, then gradually combine them. Try starting quietly, then building up the volume. Returning the chant to a whisper at the end is effective, especially as children are inclined to get overexcited and this returns their adrenalin to normal levels!

■ **Raps.** Rap and dub poetry is Afro-Caribbean in origin. It forms a link for many people between poetry and pop. It is sad that poetry should have been divorced from popular culture in the first place. The basis of it is rhythmic speech to music. This is, of course, not new, nor limited to one culture; 'Facade' by William Walton and Edith Sitwell, written in the thirties, works in the same way and is highly regarded by current rap practitioners. Children enjoy it too!

Writing a rap. Rap writing works particularly well in pairs. The basic technique is to speak and perform first, then write it down when the sound is right. Martin Glynn offers some advice on writing poetry in rap.

Poetry is ... Rap

Take a P O
E T
R and Y
Pencil and paper
The words will fly
Like spittin' from yer mouth
Aim in a direcshun
Movin' in a circle
Just like convecshun
Yer can't critisize
The size of a poem
Some are dull
Others are glowin'
Wurdz transfushan
A sentence injecshun
You can't stop
A poems infecshun
RAP
RHYME
RHYTHM
BEAT
SHORT
FAT
THIN
No idea
Can't begin
Puttin' brain power
To the test
Once you've started
You can't rest
WHISPER
SCREAM IT
SHOUT IT
SING
YER WURDZ EXPRESS
ANYTHING
The wurdz to a beat
Or no structure
Once you start
The poems GOTCHA

Can't escape
From what it's sayin'
Poetry knows
The game you're playin'
The flow, goes slow
Sometimes fast
Sometimes lingers
Doesn't last
SHORT
FAT
LONG
THIN
FUNNY
AND SERIOUS
PAINFUL
EMMOSHUNAL
SOOTHIN'
AND DELIRIOUS
INSPIRASHUN
PERSPIRASHUN
WORKING ON A POEM
IS FRUSTRASHUN
Style, form, length
Subject matter
Just like a fish
You will batter
The life out of a sentence
Strangle the syllable
Choke the verb
The feelings unbearable
1st draft, 2nd draft
Then you edit
Smile on yer face
Then take credit
Yer read it back
Yer eyes start glowin
When yer realise
Yer've just done a
POEM

Martin Glynn

Iambics. *To follow rapping with the Iambic Pentameter would appear to be a huge and bizarre cultural jump. Not so: they both represent attempts to exploit the 'hypnosis effect' of rhythmic speech. An Iambic line, very simply, is a line that alternates stressed and non-stressed syllables, starting with a non-stressed syllable. Stressed syllables are marked with a* /.

I saw a man whose face was painted green.

An Iamb is a non-stress followed by a stress - **de DUM**. *Iambic Pentameter is simply five Iambs -* **de DUM de DUM**, **de DUM de DUM de DUM**, *with a pause in the middle.*

■ *Writing an iambic line.* *Start by clapping the rhythm -* **de DUM de DUM de DUM de DUM de DUM**, *then set this line to be completed using that rhythm:*

*I saw, a man, who (***DUM de DUM de DUM***).*

Once the children are familiar with the pattern, they can start accumulating lines. The following example was a class poem, worked out on the chalkboard. It may seem odd and slightly archaic - but it works!

The rain poured down and splattered on the ground,
I gazed forlorn on cold and glossy streets:
I felt so sad I thought I'd go to bed!
Then thunder clapped and made the clouds roll back,
The lightning flashed and struck across the sky,
The sun came out and dried up all the rain;
Now the sun has set, and soon the moon appears.

TELLING STORIES

The insistance on formality in story telling often gets the result it deserves; stilted writing with cliched characters and situations with little relevance to the writer's own situation. Both the informality of poetry and, conversely, its patterning and structure, can liberate story-telling in school.

'Free verse' doesn't mean writing that is arbitrary and unstructured. Rather, it allows the poet to seek out the structure most appropriate for the job in hand. The form mirrors the subject. In all too much story writing, the writer is locked in to a formal structure. A 'beginning' is required ... One day ... and a conclusion ... we went home.

Children are, in fact, actually very good story-tellers, both in telling about real incidents in their own lives, and in weaving fantasies. Shaking off the formality of the story allows this talent to come through.

Creepy stories. Here is the opening of a poem based on that done-to-death story, entering a haunted house:

The door
C R E A K E D

S
 L
  O
   W
    L
     Y
Open

Inside was a hall,
A dark,
dusty,
damp,
M O U L D Y
hall,
With
Batsandspidersandrats
Flapping
and
Creeping
and
Scuttling
About.

Then,
faintly,
In the distance,
I heard
the sound
of
Footsteps ...

is worth looking closely at this poem with the class and discussing the various devices employed. The tension builds through short lines and repetitions. Other tricks, such as running words together, add to the unfolding horror. As an initial exercise, children might like to continue this story. Alternatively, they could devise a 'creepy' poem of their own. Possibilities are:

- The old attic
- The ghosty graveyard
- Exploring a cave or castle
- The school at night
- Coming downstairs for a forbidden midnight feast in the kitchen.

■ **More formal patterns.** Variations on ballad metre are a popular traditional form for telling stories. I suggest some work on ballads as the basis for drama later in this book (page 82). The traditional ballad pattern is the simple four-line stanza, second and fourth lines rhyming, alternating four feet and three:

From The Ballad of Chevy Chase

God prosper long our noble king,
Our lives and safety all!
A woeful hunting once there did
In Chevy Chase befall.

Suggesting that children try this pattern might seem to contradict all that has gone before. Surely we are trying to move away from cliched rigidity? Having a go at ballad metre is something new for children, unlike the formal story, which they are writing all the time.
- The formal structure of the ballad doesn't impose limitations on the content of the story, in the way that the 'story' seems to.
- Ballad metre works well for story-telling, as story-tellers have found over the centuries, because of is memorability - essential in an oral tradition. It is a medium appropriate for the job in hand.
- Formal pattern does not have to be restricting. Children enjoy the challenge of limitations put upon them.
- The main problem is that it is difficult for young writers to sustain, so any attempt in this medium should be kept short. Metrical regularity is an aim, but not an essential; the roughness of many old ballads is part of their character.

The Group Ballad. The whole class can contribute towards this! After reading some ballads and talking about what makes them special give children a slightly unusual story - perhaps a folk tale they will not have heard before, or a fairy story from another culture.
■ *Divide the story into chunks and allocate one per group. The groups take their section and write perhaps four ballad verses about it, using the discussed format. Afterwards the groups come together and read their poems - a ballad version of the story.*
- *Does the story hold together?*
- *Does anything not work - if not, why?*
■ *There can then be a final drafting session and the complete ballad - contributed to by everyone in the class - can be performed or presented.*

ANECDOTES

- Fantasy stories about ghosts, dinosaurs, spacemen and so on are part of the stock-in-trade of children's writing.
- These sorts of theme bring their own cliches, but perhaps this worries adults more than it should.
- After all, a cliche is another form of repetition.

It is important that children's own experiences should feature in their own writing. Unfortunately, much of this writing is consigned to something called 'news', sometimes a daily chore for children who struggle to convert real experiences - delightful, tragic, funny - into leaden prose.

Yesterday we went to the wildlife park. I saw elephants, monkeys and a giraffe. We had a picnic there. When we were coming home the car had a puncture ... and so on. News it is well named, as it sounds like headlines from a news bulletin.

One of the problems with story-telling is that we forget its origins in the oral tradition. Stories were told and listened to, not written and read.

Obviously, we cannot go back to that tradition entirely, but we can exploit it.

Oral story-telling. Sit the children in groups and ask them to remember something funny, surprising, or even disastrous that happened to them or their family recently.

■ Discuss the idea of 'It wasn't funny at the time' and how time changes the way we look at things. When they have thought of their experience, ask them to tell their story to the group.

■ Encourage other members of the group to ask the teller questions such as those below. If necessary, start this off yourself. It is important that children should be listening to the stories that are being told, not just thinking about their own stories.

- What did you/mum/dad say when this happened?
- How did you feel about it?

■ The stories can be read into a tape recorder, for later transcription. An alternative is to use writing pairs, with one telling the story and the other writing it down; the pair then change roles.

Here are some transcripts of stories told by a group of children. These are not poems, but are the raw material for narrative poems. I will deal with the process of turning them into poems in the next section.

> My Sister my Mum and my Dad went to a book fair and we saw a man who was dressed in the same clothes as Dad and when we were going to go home I said to Mum, 'Is Daddy going to buy me a book?' Mum said, 'I don't think he is.' But I went up to him and said, 'Daddy', and he turned round and everyone laughed.
>
> Jenny

> In the summer my mum was watering the garden with the hose when she had finished she put it on the grass and got a deck chair out and put it on top of the hose and sat down. Dad was round by the garage and he turned the tap on and it came out of the hose and soaked Mum. Dad laughed and we just kept quiet.
>
> Ruth

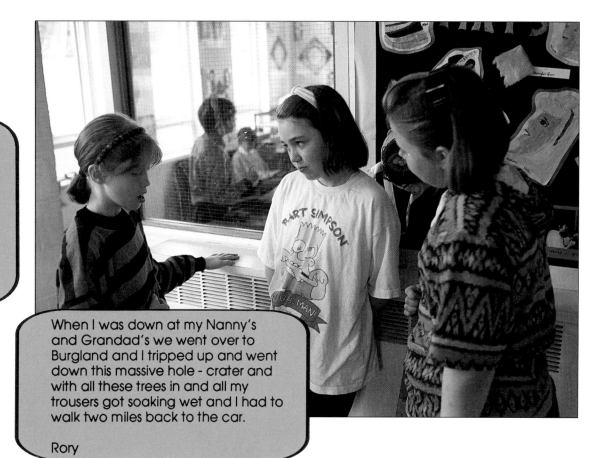

> When I was down at my Nanny's and Grandad's we went over to Burgland and I tripped up and went down this massive hole - crater and with all these trees in and all my trousers got soaking wet and I had to walk two miles back to the car.
>
> Rory

> One day before Christmas me and my mum went out shopping and when we got back we saw a black bird that had fallen down the chimney.
>
> James

Oral story-telling can be a good start for drama activities in which the children work the material up into a script or improvise. A more sophisticated approach is to turn the stories into ballads:

It was a sunny Tuesday,
Mum thought she'd use the hose,
She used it on the flower bed,
Then on the grass it goes ...

STORIES INTO POEMS

To turn anecdotes into poems requires all of the ideas and techniques discussed in this book. In particular the work on free verse and lineation (page 68) is important.

As a class, we worked on Craig's story on the board. The class asked Craig questions about his experience and he was asked to approve of the various ways in which his story was developed.

My little brother Todd has successfully learnt to climb up the settee my sister left a table next to the sofa and Todd climbed up. I went into the room to turn off the video and slipped over banged my lip and head.

Craig

Stage 1: making it clear.
It was not very clear in Craig's story what the connection was between the two events described. Craig explained that, on entering the room, he saw his baby brother climbing on the table. On rushing to his rescue he tripped and banged his head. It is important in group or pairwork that the writing partners are involved at all stages in developing the poem, particularly by asking questions.

■ **Stage 2: bringing life to the poem.** What did the various people say?

'Mum! Todd's climbing on the table.'

What noises were made?

'Ow!' 'Bang!'

Would writing in the present tense make it more exciting?

I go into the room
to turn the video off,
And I see him ...

In the end, Craig kept the poem in the past tense, but decided to use the present for the last line.

Stage 3: cutting and putting into lines.

Are there words and ideas that we need to cut out?
- Where will the lines end?
- Why?

The completed poem:

My little brother

Todd's learning to climb the settee,
And my sister Hannah left the table next to it!
Todd climbed up.

I went in to the room,
to turn the video off,
And saw him.

'Mum! Todd's climbing on the table!'
I went for him.

BANG!

OW!
I've got an aching head!

Edward worked on his 'Dirty Dishwasher' story.

Once when I came home from school I found loads of bubbles on the floor. I said to my mum what happened; she said I found that the dishwasher was dirty so I put some Fairy washing-up liquid in and turned it on and she said that she opened it up and cleared all the bubbles with a mop.

Edward

My Dirty Dishwasher

'Oh No!' said Mum.
'This dishwasher is a bit dirty.'

So she put Fairy washing-up liquid inside,
And turned it on.

When we came home from school,
There were BUBBLES and BUBBLES and BUBBLES
all over the floor.

'Oh Mum! What HAVE you done?'

■ It is perfectly permissible, of course, to exaggerate and embroider the narrative. When asked, 'What did they say?' the usual answer is, 'I don't remember!'
In this case, ask, 'What do you think they might have said?'

PERFORMANCE IDEAS

- When the poems are finished, children will be keen to present them, either by display, publication, or performance.
- The concept of audience is an important one.
- Who are we writing for?
- How can we best offer our poems to them?
- Leaving poems in an exercise book or work folder misses out on this important final stage.

I would stress again the importance of the oral element in poetry; poems need to be listened to. The simplest way to do this is for the author to read the poem out to the class.

- Unless the poet is a fluent reader, or has prepared the reading, it is unlikely to hold the attention of the class. A performance session should be seen as 'listening' practice for the class as well as 'reading aloud' practice for the poet.
- A whole series of poems read one after the other will soon bore the class.

Aim at 'performance' rather than reading aloud. These suggestions will help to give such sessions a sense of 'occasion'.

✓ The performance needs preparation and practice, especially by the less able readers.

✓ Encourage the children to work out a range of approaches, such as paired reading, sharing the lines between two speakers, choral reading, chorus poems in which the audience is invited to join in.

✓ Consider the possibility of sound effects, and even 'costume' - see the work on masks, page 46.

✓ Plan your performance so there is plenty of variety; include, perhaps, poems by adult writers.

✓ Be involved in the performance by reading some poems yourself.

✓ Find a wider audience; another class, the infants, the school, a visitor.

✓ Use audio and videotaping to preserve the performance.

Performances should not be seen as just an opportunity for presenting the writing the class has done; poems that they have particularly enjoyed reading can be included. Some poems make ideal performance pieces; some can form the basis of interesting drama work.

Ballads. Many traditional ballads work well as drama. The approach is simple. Divide the class into performers and narrators. Photocopy your ballad, then highlight the 'speaking parts' for each actor. Divide up the 'narrated' element so that the children have a small section each that they can learn by heart. The performance can be as simple, or as sophisticated, as you wish; from a class activity to a full-blown 'play'.

The following ballad works well as performance; there are many more, although be aware that the emphasis is firmly on the 'male hero', so provide balance wherever possible.

The Death of Nelson

Come all gallant seamen that unite a
meeting,
Attend to these lines I'm going to relate,
And when that you hear, it will move you
with pity
To hear how Lord Nelson, he met with his
fate.
For he was a bold and undaunted
commander,
As ever did sail on the ocean wide,
And he made both the French and the
Spaniards surrender
By always pouring into them a broadside.

From aloft to aloft, where he was
commanding,
All by a French gun he received a ball
And by the contents he got mortally wounded
And that was the occasion of Lord Nelson's
fall.
Like an undaunted hero, exposed to the fire,
As he gave the command, on the
quarter-deck stood,
And to hear of his actions, you would much
admire,
To see the decks covered all with human
blood.

One hundred engagements he had been into,
And never, in his time, was he known to be
beat,
For he had lost an arm, likewise his right eye
sir,
No powers on Earth could ever him defeat.
His age at his death, it was forty and seven,
And as long as I live, his great praises I'll sing,
For the whole navigation was given unto him
Because he was loyal and true to his king.

Then up steps the doctor in a very great hurry
And unto Lord Nelson these words he did
say,
Indeed then, my Lord, I am very sorry,
To see you lying and bleeding this way.
No matter, no matter, whatever about me,
My time it has come, I'm almost at the worst,
And there's my gallant seamen who're fighting
so boldly,
Go and discharge your duty to them first.

Then with a loud voice he called out to his
captain,
Pray let me know how this battle does go,
I think that our guns continue to rattle,
Though death approaches I very well know.

The antagonist's ship has gone to the
bottom,
Eighteen we've captured, and brought them
on board,
And here are two of them quite blown out of
the ocean,
So that is the news I have brought you, my
Lord.

Come all gallant seamen that unite a
meeting,
Always let Lord Nelson's memory go round;
For it is your duty when you unite a
meeting,
Because he was loyal and true to the
crown.
So now to conclude and to finish these
verses,
My time it is come, I am quite at the worst,
May the heavens go with you, and ten
thousand blessings,
May rest in the Fleet with you, Lord
Collingwood.

Anonymous nineteenth-century broadsheet

Various 'Robin Hood' ballads are an excellent source of material and can be linked together to make quite a substantial production. It is generally a good idea to modernise the text where possible. The production can be as simple or as elaborate as desired. Much use can be made of mime; the sailors in battle, the French sniper and so on. Dramatic lighting, if available can give splendid battle effects. Suitably nautical costumes can be devised.

DISPLAY

Poetry can form an attractive element in a special 'topic' display, but allow an area where poetry can be displayed on its own merits. Poetry is frequently presented in neat, regimented rows of identically sized pieces of paper. This is dull and does not attract the potential reader. Other more imaginative possibilities are:

■ **Window poems.** These can be written on transluscent paper or film and attached to the window. You could try a stained glass window display.

The Poem tree (or Poetree). Poems can be written on different sizes, shapes and colours of paper, and places in the tree as leaves or fruit. The tree can be simply painted on paper, cut and mounted on a wall. To make a three-dimensional tree, branches can be used. Why not include Christmas poems as part of the decoration for a Christmas tree? Christmas decorations themselves can be improved if poems are written on them.

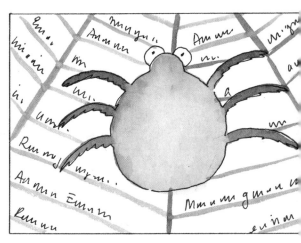

■ **The poetry spider.** The topic can be written on the spider in the centre of the display, and the poems themselves trapped in the web surrounding it. The web can be drawn or made from wool. This is particularly good for a horror display!

Poetry collage. A wall display illustrating a particular theme can incorporate poems. On page 31 there is a simple goldfish display, with goldfish poems written on the goldfish. You can try a more ambitious display, showing an undersea world. Other possibilities include a busy street, a forest, a space scene, a snow scene, an airport or a station.

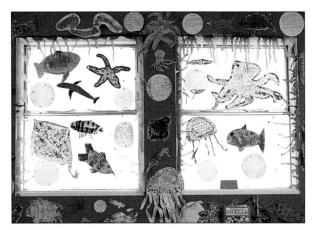

Work in progress. A board displaying drafts of poems in progress. The poets can ask for help and suggestions! When the final poem is finished, this can be displayed along with the drafts.

■ **Ceiling poems.** Allow poems to hang from the ceiling! Of course paper will soon curl, and so three-dimensional poems are best. These can be simple shapes or can be the shape of the subject of the poem.

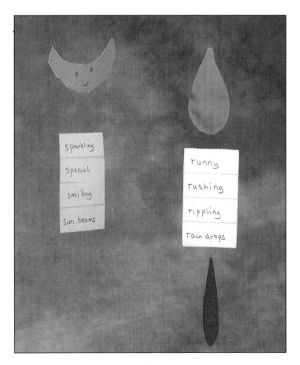

■ **Hidden poems.** These intrigue the reader by hiding all or part of the poem. The simplest is to place a door over the poem displayed by placing a piece of paper over it and stapling at one side. On the door can be written an invitation to read the poem within. Even more fun is to write a riddle or a poem with a surprise ending and conceal just the answer or final lines. A riddle box is a small paper box with the riddle on the lid and the answer (or the object itself, or a picture of it) inside.

PUBLISHING

- By publishing I mean producing more than one copy of a poem or poems, as a booklet or broadsheet.
- This will, almost inevitably, mean using the photocopier.

A computer can print multiple copies, but this is a slow process and the results are difficult to bind in an attractive way. Photocopied pages look far more attractive than older methods of reproduction, and can include artwork, but are more expensive to produce per sheet. For class use a simple broadsheet 'Poetry Newspaper' featuring a range of poems by the class can be produced from time to time quite inexpensively.

For a prestigious school production, the cost problem can be solved by:
- Persuading a local business to sponsor the publication, or to advertise in it.
- Selling the publication to parents and friends.

A combination of these things can result in a project that actually raises funds.

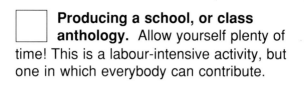

Producing a school, or class anthology. Allow yourself plenty of time! This is a labour-intensive activity, but one in which everybody can contribute.

■ **Selecting and editing.** Make this a class activity, but try and ensure everyone is included, even if the contribution is small. An oral story from even the weakest children can be written down and included.

■ **Typing up.** This need not be done in a final format, as the poems can be cut out and pasted on to the master pages, with artwork. Involve children in typing up, using the computer, and with proof-reading the poems. This is where the word processor really comes into its own, as errors can be easily corrected without the need for retyping the whole poem. Try and design a really attractive cover, perhaps using the design facilities available on your computer.

■ **Pasting up.** Another job that can involve the class. The simplest format is A4, although A5 can look attractive. If you opt for A5 with a staple in the spine you will have to work out which page should be pasted next to which in the final booklet, this is very easy to get wrong! Don't cram the pages; allow some space round each poem.

■ Running off. The most tedious and frustrating part of the job. Make sure before you start that the machine can cope with printing both sides of a piece of paper without regular indigestion. Don't leave the copying to the last minute: the machine will inevitably break down half-way through. Using your local teacher's centre may cost more, but with sophisticated machines and the availability of technicians this may be better for your blood pressure! Choose a different coloured paper for your cover and endpage, or use light card.

■ Collating and stapling. The best way is to ask the class to walk round and round a table, picking up one page at a time. Have two children to check that they haven't missed a page or picked up two by mistake. Operate the stapler yourself; children reduce staplers to wreckage very quickly. You will need a long-arm stapler if you are producing an A5 booklet stapled down the spine.

■ Official presentation. Give the publication a good send off! Invite celebrities such as a school governor to a launch party. Send a copy to the local press. All these activities can be developed and worked at by the class as a part of the wider educational process.

BOOK-MAKING

- **Children thoroughly enjoy producing their own books of poems.**
- **These may be individual collections, collections of two children working together, or even group collections.**

The suggestions on these pages are only a few of the possibilities. Encourage interesting and imaginative titles - 'My Poems' is pretty dull! Look at the titles of published collections in the classroom library. Using the title of one of the poems is a possibility; 'What My Cat Did, and other poems, by Sarah Smith'.

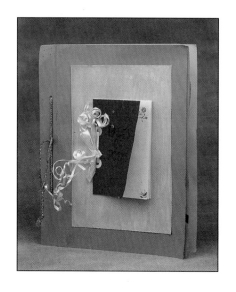

Scrap books. These are simply sheets of coloured paper or card, bound together by stapling, ring binding, tying, or long plastic paper grips. It is possible to mount and decorate poems on the pages thus created. The pages from Kelly Smith's collection, from Hothfield Junior School, show what is possible. Kelly has used felt cut-out insects and real knitting!

■ **Paper sculpture.** These make imaginative additions to poems in scrap books. They involve the reader actively in the poems. Reading a 'What's Cooking' poem might involve the lifting of a saucepan lid, which draws the poem out of the pot! Pulling a string might unfold a paper lantern on which is written the poem, or the answer to a riddle. Paper fasteners can be used for poems that swivel. Poem Fans are a good way for presenting 'Hot Day' poems. Many origami techniques provide the basis for unusual ways of presenting poems.

Zigzag or Concertina books.
These are very simple to make, and can be made as long as is needed to tell a story. Poem and picture can appear on alternating pages, either written directly on to the paper or glued on. It is important to draft the poem first and plan what goes on each page.

■ **Mini-books.** These may contain only one poem, with perhaps a line or two on each page. Mini-books are good for story poems where the need to turn the page adds to the excitement. They are simply made by folding a piece of A4 paper and stapling and cutting along the folds; more adventurous possibilities include unusual shapes for the pages. If the back cover is left blank then the books can be mounted to make a display.

■ **Shape books.** Once a book is made, a shape can be drawn on the front and the whole book cut to that pattern, taking care not to cut the binding.

USING THE MICRO

● The most important use for the micro in language work is word processing, and, increasingly these days, desktop publishing.

The advantages of the word processor to the writer are:

✓ Drafting is simple and quick.

✓ Whole blocks of text can be moved, deleted or inserted.

✓ Spelling and other errors can be corrected quickly and easily.

✓ A 'perfect' final copy can be produced.

✓ A range of attractive possibilities can be accessed for display.

✓ Work can be conveniently stored on disc.

In the classroom, these things are of particular value to the pupil, particularly the less able for whom the normal writing and rewriting process causes many problems. In addition, the computer offers many possibilities for group work; the text entered is easily visible to all members of the group. Many classrooms will have only one machine, but even this can be of value.

As far as poetry is concerned, the high level of drafting and 'playing around with words' involved is ideally suited to the word processor. One drawback to the easy production of drafts is that drafts disappear - instantly! Indeed, writing becomes less a series of discrete stages, more a continuous process. Scholars in years to come will have very little drafting material to study! It is well worth suggesting that 'snapshots' of material from the drafting process are printed out from time to time.

The more sophisticated and powerful word processors will often contain spelling checkers; even thesauruses are available, although as far as I am aware no rhyming dictionary yet exists as a computer database. Spelling checkers have their limitations - they have no grammar, and would accept 'There is to much' as valid. They are useful, though, for picking up typing errors.

```
123456789:;<=>?@ABCDEFGHIJKLMNOPQRSTUVW          10C8  20 54 4F 52 4E 20 4F 46   TORN OF
23456789:;<=>?@ABCDEFGHIJKLMNOPQRSTUVWX          10D0  46 21 22 3A 6D 25 3D 31   F!":m%=1
3456789:;<=>?@ABCDEFGHIJKLMNOPQRSTUVWXY          1058  2D 36 30 4D 24 3D 22 4F   -60M$="O
456789:;<=>?@ABCDEFGHIJKLMNOPQRSTUVWXYZ          1060  55 43 48 21 21 22 3A E7   UCH!!":.
56789:;<=>?@ABCDEFGHIJKLMNOPQRSTUVWXYZ[          1068  51 3C 2D 31 30 30 4D 24   Q<-100M$
6789:;<=>?@ABCDEFGHIJKLMNOPQRSTUVWXYZ[\          1070  3D 22 48 41 52 44 20 49   ="HARD I
789:;<=>?@ABCDEFGHIJKLMNOPQRSTUVWXYZ[\]
89:;<=>?@ABCDEFGHIJKLMNOPQRSTUVWXYZ[\]^          0028  00 00 00 00 00 00 00 00   ........
9:;<=>?@ABCDEFGHIJKLMNOPQRSTUVWXYZ[\]^           0030  00 00 00 00 00 00 00 00   ........
:;<=>?@ABCDEFGHIJKLMNOPQRSTUVWXYZ[\]^_           0038  00 00 00 00 00 00 00 00   ........
;<=>?@ABCDEFGHIJKLMNOPQRSTUVWXYZ[\]^_            0040  00 00 00 00 00 00 00 00   ........
<=>?@ABCDEFGHIJKLMNOPQRSTUVWXYZ[\]^_`at          0048  00 00 00 00 00 00 00 00   ........
=>?@ABCDEFGHIJKLMNOPQRSTUVWXYZ[\]^_`abc          0050  00 00 00 00 00 00 00 00   ........
                                                 0058  00 00 00 00 00 00 00 00   ........
0CD0  22 44 4F 57 4E 22 47 24   "DOWN"G$
0CD8  3D 22 20 55 50 20 22 8B   =" UP ".          1038  22 56 65 72 79 20 6E 69   "Very ni
0CE0  47 24 3D 22 44 4F 57 4E   G$="DOWN          1040  63 65 21 22 3A E7 51 3C   ce!":.Q<
1290  29 3E 31 38 4D 24 3D 22   )>18M$="
1298  42 52 45 41 4B 49 4E 47   BREAKING
12A0  20 55 50 21 22 3A 21 0D   UP!":!.
12A8  04 60 05 E1 0D FF ** **   .`......
>RUN
0D00  3D 22 4F 55 54 22 46 24   ="OUT"F$
0D08  3D 22 49 4E 20 22 3A 73   ="IN ":s
0D10  3D 32 30 30 20 8B 46 24   =200 .F$
0D18  3D 22 4F 55 54 22 3A 73   ="OUT":s
1090  03 F2 53 E7 94 5A 25 3E   ..S..Z%>
1098  38 4D 24 3D 22 53 43 52   8M$="SCR
10A0  41 50 45 44 20 50 4F 44   APED POD
```

Text handling programs. A range of software is available which sets up, or allows the teacher to set up, text frameworks within which the pupil can work. Prediction and cloze procedure, for example are suited to the way the computer works; some programs provide vocabulary 'on the move'. Beware though, of closed responses. Poetry is not about right or wrong answers.

Other programs provide random words. Why wait an infinity for monkeys to produce a new Shakespeare play when a computer can do it for you much more quickly! View programs that claim to write poems with scepticism, but use them as a fun activity to add variety to your poetry work.

■ **Groupwork.** It is important to keep an eye on groups and ensure that the children take turns in a fair way. The 'scribe' will key in the ideas of the group. At first, when keyboarding skills are fairly basic, impatient members of the group will attempt to take over; this should be outlawed! Keyboarding confidence will come very quickly.

Many computers have a button to reset the machine, wiping out everything in the memory. It is a good idea to temporarily disable this - if possible!

Desktop publishing (DTP). These programs take word processing a stage further by dealing with the final layout and presentation. They can offer a range of fonts (typefaces) and can print in varying sizes. Pictures or other graphics can be included, and text made to 'flow' around them. Text can be boxed, given a tint, or even reversed out onto black. In short, anything available to the professional book and magazine publisher can be available to a lesser degree in the classroom. Discs of graphics of various sorts can be obtained, including borders and other embellishments. A standard dot-matrix printer can produce attractive results, but increasingly, schools have access to laser printers that can produce professional quality print-out, and even colour printers.

The possibilities of all this for display work are enormous. The danger is, of course, in being bewitched by the technology into thinking that the original work is better than it is!

A SCHOOL POETRY FESTIVAL

- A poet's visit makes a very special highlight to a poetry week.

There are, of course, cost implications; poets are generally hard up and rely on school visits to supplement their income. What the poet actually does during their visit depends on the poet, and on discussions prior to the visit. Poets experienced in working in education will be used to running writing workshops, as opposed to a reading/answering questions session.

Organising a writer's visit.

✓ Locate your poet. In the United Kingdom, this can be done through your local Regional Arts Board, who publish contact lists. The Poetry Society Education Department, 21 Earls Court Square, LONDON SW5 9DE, will be helpful. Word of mouth is important; if you have not invited a poet before, ask for suggestions from colleagues in other local schools. Involve your pupils at this stage; why not let them write the invitation letter themselves?

✓ Sort out finance. There are a number of ways to finance the visit; selling anthologies, running bookshops, and so on. Ask about subsidies. Poets probably require considerable advance notice: never leave arrangements to the last minute.

✓ Plan the day carefully, in consultation with the poet, and send a timetable in advance. Make sure the poet is aware of the age range of the children. Don't try and pack too much in. Workshops are difficult to operate successfully with groups greater than class size, or for periods of less than an hour. A performance at the start of the day or a sharing session at the end can involve the whole school.

✓ The workshops should take place in a quiet environment. Check with the poet before the visit about requirements; blackboard, overhead projector, paper/pencils, coloured pencils, and so on. Some workshops work better at desks, some with children spread out on the floor.

✓ Make sure the poet is accompanied by a member of staff at all times. Visitors cannot legally accept responsibility for the behaviour or safety of children. Any workshop will require follow-up work after the visit, and of course this is impossible if a teacher has not been involved. The teacher should discuss her/his role in the workshop with the poet in advance.

✓ After the visit get children to write and thank the poet. Surprisingly, this happens very rarely.

Other festival activities. Collect together as many anthologies and collections as you can muster.

■ Make poetry displays for the entrance hall. Use books and poetry posters. Mix the children's own work with that of professionals.

■ Leave a display area blank in each room in which a workshop is to be held so that work can be mounted and displayed at the end of the day.

■ Make sure that there is a range of writing materials available and easily accessible in each workshop area: pens, pencils, coloured pencils, felt-tips, rough paper, best paper, coloured paper, card, paste, scissors, etc.

■ If the children are accustomed to using the word processor arrange to have it in the classroom.

■ Have a number of writing reference books handy; dictionaries, thesaurus, a rhyming dictionary if you have one.

■ Read favourite poems on to a tape recorder. Leave the book open beside the tape so that children can listen and read. Make your selection as wide as possible; 'classics', funny poems, sad ones, raps, dialect poems, and so on.

■ Find tapes or records to go with the theme you have chosen. When the children are beginning their rough work it is often helpful to have some space/sea/underground music playing.

■ Think of ways of using poetry across the curriculum, e.g. in maths or science. Find and display poems which add an extra dimension to the chldren's work in areas other than English.

■ Ask for favourite poems from childhood from teachers and other adults in the school. Make a display of remembered poems.

■ Produce an anthology of work done during the week.

■ Run a competition, if you feel it is an appropriate activity. Many people have reservations about running and entering poetry competitions, and they are not really suitable for younger children. However, a well-run school competition can be a useful 'opening round' to entering a national competition. The sharply competitive edge can be softened in various ways; team competitions, best illustrated poem, and so on.

■ Include some zany activities; the world's longest poem, menus for the week written in poetry, a poem with one line by everyone in the school - but don't let these take over!

■ Make sure that speaking and listening and these activities feature in your poetry week. Poetry assemblies can contain reading of favourite poems, choral speaking, children performing their own or other pupils' poems. Poetry is meant to be listened to as well as read and a 'quiet time' each day should be set aside for listening to poems well read by the teacher.

■ Organise a bookshop, if you do not have a regular school bookshop anyway.

■ Involve parents and the community wherever possible. Talk to the local library and see what they can offer.

■ If funds permit, invite an artist or calligrapher in to work with the children.

AN IMPOSSIBLE TASK?

- Assessing a poem is a difficult, some would say impossible, task.
- In one sense, poetry is about the unassessable, if we see assessment as providing a set of objective criteria against which the item to be assessed is to be judged.

The best poetry is unexpected, surprising, and unpredictable. Because it is intended to affect the reader in some way, poetry is by its nature subjective. Any assessment needs to involve the reader too! And yet I spend a good deal of my time adjudicating poetry competitions. How can judgements be made, one poem against another? What process is taking place? What criteria am I using? What marks out a winner from the also ran? Like all adjudicators I have spoken to, the 'tingle factor' is at the heart of any judgement. Suddenly there is a poem that makes you sit up and take notice. What makes this happen?

At the heart of a good poem is the poet's unique view of the world. The most beautifully crafted sonnet is merely an exercise if it does not cast a new light on some aspect of life or experience. When eight-year-old Russell Churcher wrote:

> Even the winter leaves
> Have their own, secret, colours.

we can share in this moment of insight. This cannot be graded or given a mark out of ten, but it is the main constituent of the 'tingle factor'. If, as a teacher, we think, 'I would never have looked at it in that way', or, 'I would never have thought of that', then poetry is at work.

What Russell Churcher has done, of course, is to relate the world of the outside to the world of human experience, and provided a metaphor for the idea that within even the most dreary of places and desperate situations there is hope. I am not suggesting for one minute that he thought all this through in an analytical way. What I am suggesting is that he felt it as an emotion, and we can share it.

Many of the ideas in this book are activities which will not produce real poems - although sometimes they do. I make no apologies for offering such activities. The craft side of writing needs to be worked on. Perceptions, insights, need the disciplines of language if they are to be communicated to others. Poets need a range of skills in order to match the language to the experience. They need to practise and practise until the skills become instinctive, never forced. No poet thinks, 'I'll just pop a bit of alliteration there!' The poet just writes the poem, and often finds to his or her surprise that various language tricks have sneaked into the poem. The language of a poem has to 'feel right'. Sometimes it is difficult to say why it is so:

> The winter leaves
> Have secret colours of their own

says much the same thing as the original poem, but the 'tingle' has gone.

The following questions are offered as a way in to looking at children's poetry. It is not an exhaustive list, and should not in any case be considered as a checklist of items to tick off. The best advice is: read, write and enjoy poetry yourself, and look out for the tingle! Do differentiate between exercises and 'writing for real'.

- Is the poem based on real experience, or related to it in some way?
- Does the poem look at its subject in a new way, perhaps through unexpected relationships?
- Has the poet chosen an appropriate pattern for the poem?
- Does the language match the theme?
- Does every word count?
- Have you read it out to the class? What do they feel about it?
- How does the poet feel about the poem?
- Did you feel a tingle?

At the end of the day, it is not important whether a child has written a good or less good poem, or even a poem at all. What is important is that:

- the child should be developing increasing confidence in handling language
- the child should be looking in an increasingly thoughtful, individual way at the world.

What is most important, though more difficult to assess, is the teacher's own enthusiasm and confidence in working with poetry. As with any subject, an enthusiastic teacher will produce an enthusiastic class.

- **Resources.** *Does your classroom have a range of poetry resources, including:*
  - *anthologies*
  - *tapes*
  - *posters*
  - *poetry cards*
  - *work by other children?*

Are the poems:
  - *classics as well as contemporary work*
  - *serious as well as funny*
  - *in a variety of forms and patterns?*

- **Writing.** *Do you:*
  - *provide a range of challenging approaches and frameworks to writing that fully stretch the children*
  - *encourage children to look for writing opportunities in their own lives*
  - *present writing as a real activity, by asking professional writers to visit your school, and by showing the class a poet's own drafts*
  - *write yourself, and share with the class your successes and failures?*

- **Management.** *Do you:*
  - *see writing as a process starting with brainstorming, moving to drafting, then on to presentation*
  - *vary the approach to writing by working sometimes with the class, sometimes using groups or pairs, and sometimes asking children to work individually*
  - *feel confident with conferencing?*

Written by Fiona Grade

- **Speaking and Listening.** *Do you:*
  - *encourage children to read aloud and perform poems, including their own*
  - *work on performance skills, including your own*
  - *read aloud a wide range of poems*
  - *use poetry in your drama work?*

- **Presentation.** *Do you:*
  - *see awareness of an audience as an essential part of writing, rather than just an attractive add-on at the end*
  - *offer a range of possibilities for presenting written material - individual anthologies, posters, display*
  - *encourage children to word process*
  - *use tape and video*
  - *find audiences for the work of your class - other children, the whole school, parents*
  - *sometimes ask your class to write specifically for an audience, e.g. younger children?*

ACKNOWLEDGEMENTS

Photography by James and Duncan of Stills except where stated. Our thanks to the staff and children Hiltingbury Junior School, Hampshire and to Chris Webster, Tim Mason and their respective BFPO schools.

Photograph of Martin Glynn in a school's poetry workshop, courtesy of the author.

Children's Games by Pieter Breughel the Elder (c.1515 - 69) Kunsthistorisches Museum, Vienna and the Bridgeman Art Library, London.

Illustration by Valeria Petrone, Andrea Gee and the children of Hiltingbury Junior School. Illustrations for Alistair Reid's sound poems by courtesy of Ward Lock Educational from *Other Worlds*.

Cover design by Sandra Buchanan Design Associates.

The publishers would like to thank the following for permission to reproduce material:

The children of Hiltingbury Junior School for all their wonderful poetry.

David Orme for his own work.

Page 6 quotation from Ted Hughes in *Listening to Poetry*, Stanley Thornes (Publishers).

Snails from *The Penguin Book of Oral Poetry* and The American Folklore Society, University of Texas Press.

Page 9 quotation from Joan Barker in *Poetry 0-16* courtesy of *Books For Keeps*.

Page 12 quotation from D Graves *Writing: Teachers and Children at Work*, Heinemann Publishers (Oxford) Ltd.

Louis Fidge for his ideas about children working in groups.

Pilkington Glass for the Humpty Dumpty advertising poem.

Page 23 quotation by Morag Styles in *Poetry 0-16* courtesy of *Books For Keeps*.

Ray Barker for his ideas on haiku and conversation poems as first published in *Schools Poetry Review Four and Nine* (1985).

Pages 25 and 37 quotations by Adrian Ingham in *Poetry 0-16* courtesy of *Books For Keeps*.

Pages 31, 33 and 35 quotations by Cathy Pompe in *Poetry 0-16* courtesy of *Books For Keeps*.

Trevor Millum for *Ten Little Schoolchildren*, copyright Trevor Millum, published in *Too Much Schooling Can Damage Your Health* (Nelson).

They Have Yarns by Carl Sandburg from *The People Yes* by Carl Sandburg, copyright 1936 Harcourt Brace Jovanovich Inc. and renewed 1964 by Carl Sandburg, reprinted by permission of the publisher.

Moira Andrew for her Tissue box World idea

In the Station of the Metro by Ezra Pound, by permission of Faber and Faber Ltd.

The Sea and *Giant Thunder* copyright James Reeves from *The Wandering Moon and Other Poems* (Puffin Books) by James Reeves. Reprinted by Permission of the James Reeves Estate.

Girls Planting Paddy by Konishi Raizan from *The Penguin Book of Japanese Verse*, translated by Bownas and Thwaite (Penguin Books 1964), copyright Geoffrey Bownas and Anthony Thwaite, 1964.

here's a little mouse) and by e.e. cummings by permission of MacGibbon and Kee an imprint of Harper Collins Publishers Limited. Reprinted from IS 5 poems by E. E. Cummings, Edited by George James Firmage, by permission of Liveright Publishing Corporation. Copyright © 1985 by E. E. Cummings Trust. Copyright 1926 by Horace Liveright. Copyright © 1954 by E. E. Cummings. Copyright © 1985 by George James Firmage.

Sound poems by Alistair Reid from *Ounce, Dice, Trice*, copyright of the author.

Poetry is ... Rap by Martin Glynn, copyright of the author.

Kelly Smith for her poetry book.

The publishers have made every effort to contact copyright holders but this has not always been possible. If any have been overlooked we will be pleased to make any necessary arrangements.